QUINTESSENTIAL

Quinoa Desserts

QUINTESSENTIAL

Quinoa Desserts

—ABIGAIL R. GEHRING—

Eat Great, Lose Weight, Feel Healthy

SKYHORSE PUBLISHING

Skyhorse Publishing books may be purchased in bulk at special discounts for sales promotion, corporate gifts, fund-raising, or educational purposes. Special editions can also be created to specifications. For details, contact the Special Sales Department, Skyhorse Publishing, 307 West 36th Street, 11th Floor, New York, NY 10018 or info@skyhorsepublishing.com.

Skyhorse® and Skyhorse Publishing® are registered trademarks of Skyhorse Publishing, Inc.®, a Delaware corporation.

Visit our website at www.skyhorsepublishing.com.

10 9 8 7 6 5 4 3 2 1

Library of Congress Cataloging-in-Publication Data

Gehring, Abigail R.
  Quintessential quinoa desserts / Abigail R. Gehring.
     pages cm
  Includes index.
  ISBN 978-1-62914-494-8 (alk. paper) -- ISBN 978-1-63220-099-0 (Ebook)
  1. Desserts. 2. Cooking (Quinoa) 3. Gluten-free diet--Recipes. I. Title.
  TX773.G3654 2015
  641.86--dc23
                              2014032203

Paperback edition ISBN: 978-1-5107-1951-4

Cover photos by Abigail R. Gehring
Printed in China

Contents

THE WHAT, WHY, AND HOW OF QUINOA

If you're buying this book, you're probably already quite familiar with quinoa. But just in case, you should know that it's pronounced kee-nwah and it's a gluten-free ancient grain now grown primarily for its seeds. The seeds are full of protein and fiber, and also contain iron, lysine (essential for tissue growth and repair), magnesium (helps control blood sugar and often alleviates migraines), riboflavin (essential for metabolic energy production), and manganese (an antioxidant). I recommend white quinoa for the recipes in this book, but feel free to experiment with black or red quinoa as well. There is no significant difference in flavor, texture, or nutrition between the varying colors.

Quinoa should always be rinsed before use. The seeds are coated with saponins, a naturally occurring type of soap that repels birds and insects. It's great for the quinoa and for the quinoa farmers, but not so great to eat.

QUINOA FLOUR

Quinoa flour is simply ground up quinoa seeds, so it's pretty simple to make on your own. You can grind in a grain mill or a little bit at a time in a coffee grinder. I recommend roasting the quinoa flour after grinding it as you'll get a richer, slightly sweeter flavor (unroasted quinoa flour has a noticeably bitter flavor) and it will be easier to digest. To do so, preheat oven to 215°F. Spread flour about ¼ to ½ inch thick on a rimmed cookie sheet and bake for 2½ to 3 hours. Remove from oven, allow to cool, and store in an airtight container in the freezer.

Many of the recipes in this book call for Quinoa Flour Mix. Used alone, quinoa flour can lead to heavy or overly crumbly results, but with a little brown rice flour and some starch, it's beautiful. Since many people choose to use quinoa because of a gluten allergy or sensitivity, this flour mix is

8

Quintessential Quinoa Desserts

gluten-free. If you don't have any issues with gluten, you could substitute the brown rice flour and starch for whole wheat or all-purpose flour.

QUINOA FLOUR MIX

Makes 6 cups.

2 cups brown rice flour
2 cups quinoa flour, roasted (see page 8)
2 cups potato starch, tapioca starch, or arrowroot powder

Mix ingredients together and store in an airtight bag or container. For long-term storage, keep in the freezer.

COOKED QUINOA SEEDS

To cook quinoa, first rinse the quinoa thoroughly. To do so, pour the quinoa into a fine mesh strainer and run water over it until there aren't any bubbles left. After it's thoroughly rinsed, place it in a saucepan with an equal amount of water and turn the heat on high. Once the water begins to boil, reduce to a simmer and cook for about 40 minutes. Many of the recipes in this book call for cool or chilled cooked quinoa. For these, you'll want to plan ahead to give your quinoa plenty of time to cool down. Remember this ratio when deciding how much quinoa to cook:

1 cup raw quinoa + 1 cup water = 3 cups cooked quinoa.

10

QUINOA FLAKES

Quinoa flakes resemble oats and can, in fact, be used as a replacement for oats in most recipes. You can buy them in many health food stores or online.

CHOOSING SWEETENERS

If using granulated sugar, look for pure cane sugar. If sugar isn't labeled as cane, it is probably made at least partially from beets—and in America, sugar beets are mostly genetically modified. Many of the recipes in this book call for natural, less processed sweeteners, such as the following.

Honey: The best honey—both for nutrition and flavor—is in its raw form. Raw honey is a powerful antioxidant and has antiviral, antibacterial, and antifungal properties. It strengthens the immune system and can fight allergies (particularly if the honey is from local bees).

Maple Syrup: Maple syrup is, well, delicious. I'm from Vermont, so I grew up tapping trees and boiling down the sap to make our liquid gold. Maple syrup doesn't rank quite as high as honey on the health scorecard, but it does have a lot of anti-inflammatory and antioxidant properties. Be sure to use 100% real maple syrup, not a syrup that's artificially flavored.

Coconut Sugar: Evaporated sap from coconut palm trees, coconut sugar has a delicate caramel flavor, similar to brown sugar. It contains many vitamins and minerals and less fructose than cane sugar.

What about Agave? Agave, sometimes called "the great Mexican aloe," produces a sweet sap, or nectar, that is traditionally extracted from the leaves, filtered, and heated to become a concentrated syrup—sort of like the tropical version of maple syrup. However, most agave sweeteners you can find in stores come from the blue agave plant, and rather than the sap being extracted from the leaves, it comes from the starchy root bulb. The agave glucose is converted to syrup through an enzymatic and chemical process that is similar to how cornstarch is converted to high fructose corn syrup (HFCS) and results in a product that's very high in fructose. Fructose in highly concentrated forms wreaks havoc on your liver and can result in long-term health problems.

GLUTEN-FREE BAKING

Going gluten-free is a whole lot easier now than it ever has been before. Unfortunately though, many gluten-free products are not particularly healthy. Many are comprised mainly of starches and gums that are basically devoid of nutrition and saturated with unhealthy oils and lots of processed sugars. They may be "safe," but they're far from nourishing. My goal in this cookbook is to provide recipes for desserts that are safe for those avoiding gluten and relatively nutritious and definitely delicious for anyone. Though some starches and gums are helpful for holding baked goods together in the absence of gluten, the focus of these recipes is on using quinoa with a variety of whole grains and nut flours.

It takes some time to recognize which ingredients are safe and which are not. Wheat, rye, and barley are the gluten-laden culprits you must avoid.

14

Unfortunately, that's not as simple as it sounds, since those three grains show up in a myriad of forms.

Danger List: Ingredients That Contain Gluten

Barley, barley malt, barley extract
Bran
Bread flour
Bulgur wheat
Cereal
Durum
Einkorn
Farina
Farro
Gluten
Graham flour
Kamut
Malt extract, malt flavoring, malt syrup
Matzo
Rye
Semolina
Spelt*
Sprouted wheat
Wheat, wheat berry, wheat bran, wheat germ, wheat grass, wheat starch, wheat berries

*Spelt is an ancient variety of wheat, so it is not safe for individuals with celiac disease and is not used in any recipes in this book. However, some people with gluten-sensitivity or intolerance find that they can tolerate spelt just fine.

The below ingredients do not always contain gluten, and when they do, it's trace amounts. But, especially if you have celiac disease, you should be careful about what brand of the following items you are buying. Look for ones that are specifically labeled "gluten-free." For a longer list, check out www.celiac.com.

Maybe List: Ingredients That May Contain Gluten

Alcohol
Artificial color
Baking powder
Brewer's yeast
Chocolate
Dextrin
Dextrimaltose
Dry-roasted nuts
Flavoring and flavor extracts
Glucose syrup
Gravy cubes
Ground spices
Instant coffee
Maltose
Miso
Modified food starch
Non-dairy creamer
Oats, oat bran, oat fiber, oat syrup*
Rice malt
Rice syrup, brown rice syrup**
Seitan
Soba noodles
Soy sauce
Stock cubes
Teriyaki sauce
Vegetable broth

*Oats do not actually contain gluten, but are often processed in facilities that also process wheat. Look for certified gluten-free oats to ensure they're safe.
**Rice syrup is often processed using barley enzymes. Check with the manufacturer to ensure the brand you use is safe

Quintessential Quinoa Desserts

And now for the good news. Here are the exciting grains and starches that are gluten-free! To be sure your grains are not processed in facilities that also process wheat or other unsafe grains, still look for those specifically labeled "gluten-free."

Safe List: Grains That Don't Contain Gluten

Agar-agar
Almond flour
Amaranth
Arrowroot flour or starch
Buckwheat flour
Cashew flour
Chestnut flour
Chickpea/garbanzo flour
Coconut flour
Cornmeal and cornstarch
Flaxseeds
Gelatin
Millet flour
Oats (if they're certified gluten-free)
Pecan flour
Potato flour
Potato starch
Quinoa
Rice flour, brown rice flour, sweet rice flour
Sorghum
Soy flour
Sweet potato/yam flour
Tapioca flour and tapioca starch
Teff flour
Xanthan gum

Tips for Successful Gluten-Free Baking

- Use a mix of flours and starches. On page 9 you'll find a basic recipe for a gluten-free quinoa flour mix. Using a variety of flours and starches helps to ensure a nice texture in your finished dessert. Gluten-free flours and starches are fairly easy to find these days in bigger grocery stores, health food stores, or online. If you wish, use a little sweet rice flour in your flour mix—it adds some "stickiness" to your batter or dough that is sometimes lacking in gluten-free flours. I recommend brown sweet rice flour (rather than white), since it's a bit more nutritious. (Note: Sweet rice flour is sometimes called "sweet rice glutinous flour," but it doesn't contain any gluten.)

- Go small. Smaller cakes, muffins, and cookies hang together more easily than really big ones.

- Add moisture. Applesauce, pumpkin puree, and yogurt add moisture and nutrition to gluten-free baked goods. Using brown sugar instead of white also helps, as does using a little honey, maple syrup, or gluten-free brown rice syrup.

- Chill your cookie dough. Gluten-free cookie dough tends to spread out a lot. This will happen less if you drop your cookie dough onto the pan and then stick the whole pan in the refrigerator for half an hour or so before baking.

- Darker baking pans will lead to better browning.

- Store your baked goods in the refrigerator or freezer to keep them from getting stale.

- One man's baking disaster is another man's gorgeous trifle. There are plenty of good uses for baked goods that fall apart, including trifles and cake pops!

QUINTESSENTIAL

Quinoa Desserts

Cookies, Bars, and Candies

No-bake Carob Cookies

Makes about 2 dozen.

In a medium saucepan, heat the coconut oil, honey, and carob powder, stirring until fully combined. Remove from heat and add the peanut butter and vanilla, and stir. Add the cooked quinoa and mix until combined.

Line a baking sheet with parchment paper and drop tablespoon-sized dollops of batter onto it. Press the cookies down a little to flatten. Freeze for at least an hour.

4 cups cooked quinoa
¼ cup coconut oil
¼ cup honey
½ cup unsweetened carob powder
½ cup peanut butter
1 teaspoon vanilla

Perfect for a hot day when you don't want to turn on the oven but want a sweet treat, these cookies are as healthy as they are delicious. If desired, toss in a half cup of chocolate chips, dried fruit, or coconut flakes to the batter.

Vegan Pumpkin Brownies

Makes one 9 x 13-inch pan.

Preheat the oven to 350°F. Grease a 9 x 13-inch baking pan. In a medium size mixing bowl, stir together the flours, sugar, cocoa powder, baking powder, and salt. Pour in juice, vegetable oil, pumpkin puree, applesauce, and vanilla. Mix until well blended.

Spread evenly in baking pan. Sprinkle chocolate chips evenly over the top.

Bake for 25 to 30 minutes or until the top is no longer shiny. Let cool for at least 10 minutes before cutting into squares.

1 cup quinoa flour mix (page 9)

1 cup oat flour

1 cup white sugar

¾ cup unsweetened cocoa powder

1 teaspoon baking powder

1 teaspoon salt

1 cup fruit juice (apple is great, but any variety will do)

¼ cup vegetable oil

1 cup pumpkin puree

½ cup applesauce

1 teaspoon vanilla extract

1 cup dairy-free chocolate chips

Rich in flavor and low in fat, these brownies will appeal to vegans and non-vegans alike!

Quinoa Brownies

Makes 16 small brownies.

Preheat oven to 350°F and grease an
8 x 8-inch baking dish. Combine all
ingredients in a food processor and blend
until smooth.

Pour into greased pan and bake for 30 to 40
minutes, or until firm on top. Insides will
still be a bit gooey. Allow to cool slightly
before cutting.

2 cups cooked quinoa, cooled

¾ cup sugar

½ cup cocoa powder

1 teaspoon baking powder

¼ cup milk

2 tablespoons butter or coconut oil,
    melted

2 large eggs

1 teaspoon vanilla extract

For variations on these chewy brownies, toss ½
cup of chocolate chips, dried fruit, chopped nuts,
or dried coconut into the batter.

Mocha Brownies

Makes 16 small brownies.

Preheat oven to 350°F and grease an
8 x 8-inch baking dish. Combine all
ingredients except coffee granules and
chocolate chips in a food processor and
blend until smooth. Fold in coffee granules
and chocolate chips.

Pour into greased pan and bake for 30 to 40
minutes, or until firm on top. Insides will
still be a bit gooey. Allow to cool slightly
before cutting.

2 cups cooked quinoa, cooled

¾ cup sugar

½ cup cocoa powder

1 teaspoon baking powder

¼ cup milk

2 tablespoons butter or coconut oil,
    melted

2 large eggs

1 teaspoon vanilla extract

1 tablespoon instant coffee granules

¾ cup chocolate chips

Almond Butter Brownies

Makes 16 small brownies.

Preheat oven to 350°F and grease an 8 x 8-inch baking dish. Combine all ingredients in a food processor and blend until smooth.

Pour into greased pan. Heat the almond butter in the microwave or on the stovetop to soften. Use a spoon to drizzle the almond butter in stripes across the top of the batter. Cut across the batter perpendicular to the almond butter stripes, creating a swirled pattern. Bake for 30 to 40 minutes, or until firm on top. Insides will still be a bit gooey. Allow to cool slightly before cutting.

2 cups cooked quinoa, cooled

¾ cup sugar

½ cup cocoa powder

1 teaspoon baking powder

¼ cup milk

2 tablespoons butter or coconut oil, melted

2 large eggs

1 teaspoon vanilla extract

1 cup almond butter

Cream Cheese Brownies

Makes 16 small brownies.

Preheat oven to 350°F and grease an 8 x 8-inch baking dish. Combine all ingredients except cream cheese in a food processor and blend until smooth.

Pour ¾ of batter into greased pan. Spread the softened cream cheese on top and then pour the remaining brownie batter on top. Use a knife to cut back and forth across the batter to create a marbled pattern. Bake for 30 to 40 minutes, or until firm on top. Insides will still be a bit gooey. Allow to cool slightly before cutting.

2 cups cooked quinoa, cooled

¾ cup sugar

½ cup cocoa powder

1 teaspoon baking powder

¼ cup milk

2 tablespoons butter or coconut oil, melted

2 large eggs

1 teaspoon vanilla extract

4 ounces cream cheese, softened

Chocolate Quinoa Crunch

Makes about ten 1-inch square pieces.

Line a cookie sheet with parchment paper, spread quinoa on it, and bake at 350°F for 6 to 8 minutes. You're toasting the quinoa, so remove as soon as it's golden and well before it's blackened.

In a small saucepan, melt the coconut oil over low heat, add cocoa powder and honey, and stir. When fully combined, pour onto another cookie sheet lined with parchment paper. Sprinkle toasted quinoa and dried cherries evenly over the surface. Place in the freezer for at least ten minutes, or until firm. Break into pieces and enjoy immediately or store in a sealed container in the freezer.

¼ cup quinoa, raw

5 tablespoons coconut oil

5 tablespoons unsweetened cocoa powder

1 tablespoon honey

½ cup dried cherries (optional)

Making your own chocolate from coconut oil and cocoa powder is surprisingly easy! You can adjust the sweetness by adding more or less honey, and sprinkle whatever nuts, dried fruit, or seeds on top that you like.

Salted Quinoa Chocolate Bark with Pistachios

Makes about 6 servings.

Line an 8-inch pan with parchment paper. Mix melted chocolate with cayenne pepper and stir well. Pour chocolate into prepared pan and smooth with a dry spatula. Top with popped or toasted quinoa, pistachios, and sea salt.

Chill for 30 minutes, or until set. Remove from pan and break into pieces.

8 ounces good quality chocolate, melted (such as Green & Black's dark chocolate)

1/8 teaspoon cayenne pepper (optional)

1/4 cup popped quinoa (see note in box below)

1/2 cup shelled pistachios, chopped

1/4 to 1/2 teaspoon sea salt

This recipe comes from *The Gluten-Free Quintessential Quinoa Cookbook* by Wendy Polisi. To pop the quinoa, place coconut oil in a popcorn popper and allow to get warm. Add quinoa and cook about 5 minutes, until quinoa is lightly brown. Alternatively, pop the quinoa in a covered saucepan, shaking to prevent burning.

Cranberry Quinoa Cookies

Makes 2 dozen cookies.

Preheat oven to 375°F and grease 2 cookie sheets. Place dried cranberries in a bowl and cover with hot water. Allow to soak while preparing the batter.

Cream together the butter, granulated sugar, and brown sugar. Add the eggs, one at a time, beating until mixed. Add vanilla and mix.

In a separate bowl, whisk together the quinoa flour mix, baking soda, salt, and cinnamon. Add wet batter to the dry ingredients and stir to incorporate. Add quinoa flakes and stir. Drain cranberries and fold into batter.

Drop by tablespoonfuls onto greased cookie sheets. Bake for about 10 minutes or until edges are just barely golden. Remove from oven, allow to cool about two minutes, and then transfer to cooling racks. Store in an airtight container.

1 cup dried cranberries
1 cup butter, softened
1 cup granulated sugar
¾ cup brown sugar
2 eggs
1 teaspoon vanilla extract
2½ cups quinoa flour mix (page 9)
1 teaspoon baking soda
½ teaspoon salt
1½ teaspoons ground cinnamon
3 cups quinoa flakes

Quinoa flakes can be found at many health food stores or online. Whatever you don't use for baking can be cooked just like oatmeal and eaten for breakfast!

Energy Cookies

Makes 2 dozen cookies.

Soak the dates in hot water for about 5 minutes and then drain. Preheat oven to 375°F and line 2 baking sheets with parchment paper.

In the bowl of a food processor, process the dates until they become nearly paste. Add the peanut butter, chickpeas, flax seeds, milk, and vanilla, and process until smooth. Add the quinoa flour mix and baking soda and process just until mixed. Stir in chocolate chips.

Drop by tablespoonful onto cookie sheets and press down lightly with the back of a fork. Cookies will not spread, so they can be placed close together on the sheet. Bake for about 10 minutes, or until edges are lightly browned.

1 cup dried and pitted dates

½ cup peanut butter

1 can chickpeas, drained and rinsed

1 tablespoon ground flax seeds

⅓ cup milk (I used almond milk)

1 teaspoon vanilla extract

½ teaspoon baking soda

1 cup quinoa flour mix (page 9)

½ cup dark chocolate chips (optional)

These cookies came about one morning when I was feeling particularly sluggish and wanted a pick-me-up that wouldn't pull me down with a sugar crash later. Full of protein and sweetened only with dates, they were just what I needed.

Quinoa Chocolate Truffles

Makes about 35 truffles.

Line a cookie sheet with parchment paper, spread quinoa on it, and bake at 350°F for 6 to 8 minutes. The goal is to toast the quinoa, so remove as soon as it's golden and well before it's blackened.

Place the chocolate pieces in a medium-size mixing bowl. In a small saucepan, heat the cream until it begins to simmer, and then pour over the chocolate. Add the vanilla and stir until the mixture becomes smooth. Add toasted quinoa, mix, and refrigerate for about 2 hours.

Line a baking sheet with parchment paper. Remove the ganache mixture from the refrigerator. Scoop out small spoonfuls of the ganache and then roll between your palms to form smooth balls. Place on the lined baking sheet and refrigerate for another 30 minutes.

Store in the refrigerator in an airtight container.

¼ cup quinoa, raw

12 ounces semisweet or dark chocolate, chopped into small pieces

½ cup heavy cream

1 teaspoon vanilla extract

Hazelnut Rocher Truffles

Makes about 50 truffles.

Line a cookie sheet with parchment paper, spread quinoa on it, and bake at 350°F for 6 to 8 minutes. The goal is to toast the quinoa, so remove as soon as it's golden and well before it's blackened.

In a food processor, pulverize the hazelnuts. Add the Nutella and liqueur and pulse until mixed. Add toasted quinoa and pulse a few more times until mixed.

Refrigerate mixture for about 20 minutes. When firm enough to handle, form into bite-size balls. Place on a baking sheet lined with parchment paper and freeze for 10 to 15 minutes.

In a double boiler, melt the chocolate. Dip each ball in the chocolate and set on the lined tray to set. Refrigerate another 10 minutes or so before serving. Store in the refrigerator.

1 cup quinoa, raw
2 cups toasted hazelnuts
1 cup Nutella
¼ cup hazelnut liqueur (optional)
8 ounces dark chocolate, chopped

Crunchy Mocha Fudge

Makes about 16 squares.

Line a cookie sheet with parchment paper, spread quinoa on it, and bake at 350°F for 6 to 8 minutes. The goal is to toast the quinoa, so remove as soon as it's golden and well before it's blackened.

Grease an 8 x 8-inch baking pan.

In a medium saucepan, heat sweetened condensed milk and chocolate chips. Stir and heat until mixture becomes smooth. Remove from heat and add vanilla, instant coffee granules, and toasted quinoa.

Pour into pan and allow to cool until set. Slice into 1-inch squares.

¼ cup quinoa, raw

1 (14-ounce) can sweetened condensed milk

12 ounces semisweet chocolate chips

½ teaspoon vanilla extract

1 teaspoon instant coffee granules

Chocolate Peanut Butter Cups

Makes about 2 dozen candies.

Line a cookie sheet with parchment paper, spread quinoa on it, and bake at 350°F for 6 to 8 minutes. The goal is to toast the quinoa, so remove as soon as it's golden and well before it's blackened.

Mix together the peanut butter and softened butter until smooth. Add the confectioners' sugar and salt and mix. Add toasted quinoa and mix to distribute.

Melt the chocolate in a double boiler or in the microwave. Remove from heat and use a teaspoon to drop a little melted chocolate in the bottom of each candy cup. Use the brush to "paint" the inside sides of the cups with chocolate.

Scoop a little of the peanut butter mixture into each cup, and then top with more melted chocolate. Refrigerate until set.

½ cup quinoa, raw
¾ cup smooth peanut butter
3 tablespoons unsalted butter, room temperature
½ cup confectioners' sugar
¼ teaspoon salt
12 ounces chocolate, chopped
24 foil candy cups
Pastry brush

Peanut butter cups are my favorite candy, and these are even better than the store-bought varieties! The toasted quinoa adds a delightful crunch.

Pecan Quinoa Toffee

Makes about 1¾ pounds.

Line a cookie sheet with parchment paper, spread quinoa on it, and bake at 350°F for 6 to 8 minutes. The goal is to toast the quinoa, so remove as soon as it's golden and well before it's blackened.

Line a baking sheet with aluminum foil and lightly grease the foil with oil. Spread 1½ cups pecan pieces evenly over the foil.

Combine sugar, butter, water, and salt in a medium saucepan and cook over medium heat, stirring regularly. When mixture begins to boil, insert candy thermometer.

When mixture reaches 300°F (hard crack stage), pour over the pecan pieces. Sprinkle remaining pecan pieces, toasted quinoa, and chocolate pieces over the top. Allow to cool and then break into pieces.

½ cup quinoa, raw
2 cups pecans, chopped
1 cup sugar
1 cup butter, cut into tablespoons
½ teaspoon salt
¼ cup water
6 ounces chocolate, finely chopped

Quinoa Cracker Jacks

Makes 20 cups.

Preheat oven to 250°F.

Line a cookie sheet with parchment paper, spread quinoa on it, and bake at 350°F for 6 to 8 minutes. The goal is to toast the quinoa, so remove as soon as it's golden and well before it's blackened.

Pour popcorn onto the baking sheet with the toasted quinoa and cranberries or cherries. Stir with a spatula to distribute.

In a medium saucepan over medium heat, melt butter. Add brown sugar, water, and salt. When the mixture begins to bubble, set a timer and boil for 5 minutes without stirring.

Remove from heat, add baking soda and vanilla, and stir until the mixture foams. Pour the mixture over the popcorn in a thin stream, stirring with a wooden spoon to coat.

Bake for 1 hour, stirring every 15 minutes. Store up to a month in an airtight container.

1 cup quinoa, raw
6 quarts popped popcorn
 (1 cup unpopped)
1 cup dried cranberries or cherries
 (optional)
1 cup butter
2 cups packed brown sugar
1 cup water
1 teaspoon salt
1 teaspoon baking soda
2 teaspoons vanilla extract

Cookies, Bars, and Candies

Maple Quinoa Nut Brittle

Makes about 2 pounds of brittle.

½ cup quinoa, raw

2 cups roasted and salted nuts
(peanuts, pecans, or walnuts)

2 cups sugar

½ cup water

1 cup maple syrup

1 teaspoon baking soda

Line a cookie sheet with parchment paper, spread quinoa on it, and bake at 350°F for 6 to 8 minutes. The goal is to toast the quinoa, so remove as soon as it's golden and well before it's blackened. Once toasted, pour quinoa into a separate dish. Remove parchment paper from cookie sheet and grease sheet thoroughly.

In a medium saucepan, heat the sugar, water, and maple syrup. Continue at a slow boil, stirring gently, until mixture reaches 245°F. Add the nuts and stir.

When the mixture reaches 300°F, add the baking soda, stir, and remove from heat. Mixture will foam, so be careful.

Pour onto the greased pan and use a wooden spoon or spatula to spread the mixture. Sprinkle toasted quinoa evenly over the top. Cool completely before breaking into pieces.

Brittles are easy to make, but have all your ingredients ready before you start because you can't waste any time between steps. If you find that your brittle isn't hardening, you can scoop it up, return it to the saucepan, and reheat it—chances are you didn't cook it quite long enough the first time.

Cookies, Bars, and Candies

Candy-Coated Nuts

Makes 4 cups.

Line a cookie sheet with parchment paper, spread quinoa on it, and bake at 350°F for 6 to 8 minutes. The goal is to toast the quinoa, so remove as soon as it's golden and well before it's blackened. Once toasted, pour quinoa into a separate dish. Remove parchment paper from cookie sheet and grease sheet thoroughly.

Preheat oven to 275°F. Beat egg whites until stiff, add granulated sugar, brown sugar, vanilla, cinnamon, and salt and continue to beat for about a minute.

Combine mixture with nuts and toss to coat the nuts. Spread the nuts on the greased cookie sheet and bake for about 45 minutes, stirring every 15 minutes. Remove from oven and immediately pour into a bowl, add the toasted quinoa, and toss to coat. Store in an airtight container.

½ cup quinoa, raw

2 egg whites

½ cup granulated sugar

½ cup brown sugar

1 teaspoon vanilla extract

1 teaspoon cinnamon

½ teaspoon salt

4 cups raw pecan halves, peanuts, or cashews

Quinoa Halvah

Makes about 2 pounds.

Line a cookie sheet with parchment paper, spread quinoa on it, and bake at 350°F for 6 to 8 minutes. The goal is to toast the quinoa, so remove as soon as it's golden and well before it's blackened.

Lightly grease a 6-cup mold or cake pan.

Beat or stir the tahini to incorporate the oil into the sesame paste. In a medium saucepan over low heat, bring the honey to a simmer. Insert candy thermometer and heat to 240°F (soft ball stage).

Remove from heat and allow to cool to 120°F. Add the vanilla, nuts, and toasted quinoa and then the tahini and stir gently.

Pour into the greased pan, cover with plastic, and refrigerate for 24 to 36 hours.

½ cup quinoa, raw
2 cups honey
1½ cups tahini
1 teaspoon vanilla extract
1 cup nuts (almonds, pistachios, or hazelnuts), peeled and lightly toasted

Cookies, Bars, and Candies

Dried Cherry and Chocolate Balls

Makes about 2 dozen balls.

Line a cookie sheet with parchment paper, spread quinoa on it, and bake at 350°F for 6 to 8 minutes. The goal is to toast the quinoa, so remove as soon as it's golden and well before it's blackened.

Combine cherries, almond butter, honey, and coconut oil in a food processor and pulse until chopped and combined. Scoop into a large mixing bowl, add toasted quinoa, and mix. Roll mixture into 1-inch balls and set on the lined baking sheet. Refrigerate for about 30 minutes.

Melt chocolate in a double boiler. Dip each ball in the chocolate and return to the baking sheet. Refrigerate for about 30 minutes. Store in airtight container in refrigerator about 2 weeks.

1 cup quinoa, raw
1 cup dried cherries
½ cup almond butter
3 tablespoons honey
3 tablespoons coconut oil
8 ounces bittersweet chocolate, chopped

Modify this recipe to your own palate by adding other dried fruits or nuts!

Sugar Plums

Makes about 1½ cups of sugar plums.

Line a cookie sheet with parchment paper, spread quinoa on it, and bake at 350°F for 6 to 8 minutes. The goal is to toast the quinoa, so remove as soon as it's golden and well before it's blackened.

In a food processor, pulse together the dried fruit and nuts. Add the toasted quinoa and other remaining ingredients (except for the sugar) and pulse until mixture starts to clump together.

Roll the dough into small balls and roll in the sugar. Store in an airtight container between layers of waxed paper for up to a month.

½ cup quinoa, raw

¼ cup almonds, hazelnuts, or walnuts (or a mix)

¾ cup Medjool dates, prunes, dried cranberries, or raisins (or a mix)

1 tablespoon honey

3 tablespoons nut butter (almond, peanut, or cashew)

⅛ teaspoon almond extract

⅛ teaspoon vanilla extract

½ teaspoon cinnamon

⅛ teaspoon cloves

½ cup raw, coarse sugar or coconut sugar

Quinoa Date Snowballs

Makes 16 servings.

Place coconut in a shallow dish. In a food processor combine dates, quinoa, almonds, sugar, cinnamon, vanilla, and sea salt. Process until smooth.

Form into very small balls, about ½ teaspoon in size. Roll the balls in the coconut, pressing to coat as needed.

3 tablespoons unsweetened shredded coconut

5 ounces pitted dried dates

½ cup cooked quinoa

¼ cup raw almonds

1 tablespoon coconut sugar (optional)

½ teaspoon cinnamon

½ teaspoon vanilla extract

⅛ teaspoon sea salt

This recipe comes from *The Gluten-Free Quintessential Quinoa Cookbook* by Wendy Polisi.

Chocolate Quinoa Apple Wedges

Makes 8 servings.

Line a baking sheet with parchment or wax paper.

Combine lemon juice and water and add apple wedges. Toss to coat and set aside.

Heat coconut oil over medium heat. Add quinoa, oats, and coconut sugar. Toast, stirring frequently for 5 to 7 minutes or until quinoa is golden brown. Place in a shallow dish and allow to cool slightly.

Place chocolate in the top of a double boiler over low heat. Stir until melted, making sure that no water reaches the chocolate.

Drain apple wedges on a paper towel. Carefully dip apple wedges in chocolate, holding from the skin side. Alternately, you may use a spoon to spread the chocolate over the wedges, holding over the boiler to allow any excess to drip back. Place on the prepared baking sheet and sprinkle with quinoa mixture, pressing lightly so that it adheres. Refrigerate for 20 minutes, or until set. Store in the refrigerator.

1 tablespoon lemon juice

1 cup water

2 large apples, cut into wedges

1 tablespoon coconut oil

¼ cup quinoa, raw

¼ cup regular or gluten-free oats

1 tablespoon coconut sugar

6 ounces chocolate, chopped fine

This recipe comes from *The Gluten-Free Quintessential Quinoa Cookbook* by Wendy Polisi.

Blondies

Makes one 8 x 8-inch pan.

Preheat oven to 350°F and grease an 8 x 8-inch pan.

If using toasted quinoa, line a cookie sheet with parchment paper, spread quinoa on it, and bake at 350°F for 6 to 8 minutes.

Beat together the butter and brown sugar until fluffy. Add egg and vanilla and beat until combined. Add flour and salt and stir to combine before folding in chocolate chips, raisins, or toasted quinoa (if using).

Pour into greased pan and bake for 20 to 25 minutes, or until set in the middle.

¼ cup quinoa, raw (optional)

½ cup (1 stick) unsalted butter, softened

¾ cup brown sugar

1 egg

2 teaspoons vanilla extract

⅛ teaspoon salt

1 cup quinoa flour mix (page 9)

1 cup semisweet chocolate chips

½ cup raisins or other dried fruit (optional)

Blondies are one of the most versatile bar cookies you can make. Go wild with nut, fruit, or flavoring additions!

58

Raspberry Bar Cookies

Makes one 8 x 8-inch pan.

Preheat oven to 350°F and line an 8 x 8-inch pan with parchment paper.

In a medium mixing bowl, combine brown sugar, flour, baking soda, salt, and quinoa flakes or rolled oats. Add the softened butter and mix together with your fingers or two forks, until mixture resembles coarse crumbs.

Press 2 cups of the crumbly mixture into the bottom of the lined pan. Spread the jam over top and then distribute the remaining crumbly mixture evenly over the top.

Bake for 35 to 40 minutes or until topping is lightly browned. Remove from oven, cool, and then cut into squares.

½ cup light brown sugar

1 cup quinoa flour mix (page 9)

¼ teaspoon baking soda

⅛ teaspoon salt

1 cup quinoa flakes or rolled oats

½ cup butter, softened

¾ cup raspberry jam

Coconut Florentine Lace Cookies

Makes 2 dozen cookies.

Preheat oven to 350°F. Line 2 rimmed cookie sheets with foil. Grease foil and set aside.

In a medium saucepan, combine sugar, butter, coconut milk, and agave nectar. Cook over low heat for about 5 minutes or until sugar is dissolved, stirring near constantly.

Bring to a boil. To prevent sugar from crystallizing, brush down sides of saucepan with a wet pastry brush. Cook until thermometer registers 238°F. Remove from heat and immediately stir in quinoa flakes, quinoa, almonds, coconut, flour, lemon peel, and vanilla extract.

Drop by the tablespoon on prepared pans. (Keep about 3 inches apart.) With a fork dipped in cold water, flatten the cookies. Bake for 5 minutes. Switch racks and bake for 3 to 5 minutes longer.

Cool on baking sheets and then lift from foil. Place on a large sheet of parchment paper.

Place chocolate in the top of a double boiler and melt over simmering water. Stir in cayenne pepper. Drizzle cookies with chocolate and let sit until chocolate has set.

¾ cup coconut sugar

½ cup Earth Balance or butter

⅓ cup canned coconut milk

2 tablespoons agave nectar or maple syrup

½ cup quinoa flakes

½ cup cooked quinoa

1 cup finely chopped almonds

½ cup shredded unsweetened coconut

3 tablespoons quinoa flour mix (page 9)

½ teaspoon grated lemon peel

1 teaspoon vanilla extract

CHOCOLATE DRIZZLE (optional)

⅛ teaspoon cayenne pepper (optional)

4 ounces dark chocolate

This recipe comes from *The Gluten-Free Quintessential Quinoa Cookbook* by Wendy Polisi.

Apple Granola Bars

Makes 18 bars.

Preheat oven to 350°F. Combine quinoa flakes, oats, almonds, and sunflower seeds and place on a rimmed, parchment-lined baking sheet. Bake for 15 minutes, stirring halfway through.

Move to a large bowl and stir in quinoa flour, flax seeds, dried apples, and coconut.

Melt almond butter and coconut oil in a medium saucepan. Stir in honey and applesauce and cook on medium for 2 minutes. Stir in egg, vanilla, cinnamon, and sea salt.

Prepare baking sheet by covering it with parchment paper and spraying the parchment lightly with cooking spray. Press quinoa/oat mixture onto baking sheet and bake for 15 to 18 minutes, until edges are brown. Cool on a wire rack and cut into bars. Store in an airtight container.

2 cups quinoa flakes

1 cup gluten-free oats

1 cup almonds, chopped

½ cup raw sunflower seeds

1 egg

½ cup roasted quinoa flour (see page 8)

¼ cup ground flax seeds

½ cup dried apples, chopped

½ cup coconut flakes

½ cup almond butter

⅔ cup coconut oil

⅔ cup honey or agave nectar

½ cup applesauce

2 teaspoons vanilla extract

1 teaspoon ground cinnamon

¼ teaspoon sea salt

This recipe comes from *The Gluten-Free Quintessential Quinoa Cookbook* by Wendy Polisi.

Quinoa Power Bars

Makes 12 bars.

Preheat oven to 350°F. Line a rimmed baking sheet with parchment paper. Toss the quinoa flakes, cashews, and sunflower seeds and toast for 25 to 30 minutes, stirring occasionally.

Place in a large bowl and allow to cool slightly. Add in flax seeds, chia seeds, dried cherries, and chocolate chips.

In a small saucepan melt coconut oil. Add almond butter, applesauce, and maple syrup. Bring to a boil and lower heat to medium low. Cook for 3 minutes and stir in vanilla and sea salt. Pour mixture over dry ingredients and stir.

Transfer mixture to a rimmed baking sheet lined with parchment paper and press into a rectangle. Bake for 10 minutes. Allow to cool and then place into refrigerator until firm. Cut into desired shape. Drizzle with chocolate if desired.

2 cups quinoa flakes

1 cup chopped cashews

½ cup raw sunflower seeds

⅓ cup ground flax seeds

⅓ cup chia seeds

¾ cup dried cherries, chopped

½ cup carob or chocolate chips

2 tablespoons coconut oil

2 tablespoons almond butter

½ cup unsweetened applesauce

⅔ cup maple syrup

2 teaspoons vanilla extract

½ teaspoon sea salt

Optional: melted chocolate, for drizzling

This recipe comes from *The Gluten-Free Quintessential Quinoa Cookbook* by Wendy Polisi.

Lemon Bars

Makes one 9 x 13-inch pan.

Preheat oven to 350°F. Grease a 9 x 13-inch baking pan.

In a medium mixing bowl, combine the butter, 2 cups quinoa flour mix, and ½ cup sugar. Press mixture into the bottom of the baking pan and bake for about 15 minutes and remove from oven.

In a separate bowl, beat together the eggs, lemon juice, remaining 1½ cups sugar, and ¼ cup quinoa flour mix. Pour over the partially baked crust and bake for another 20 minutes. Remove from oven and allow bars to cool to firm up before cutting into squares.

1 cup butter, softened
2 cups white sugar, divided
2¼ cups quinoa flour mix, divided (page 9)
4 eggs
Juice from 2 lemons

Granola Bars

Makes one 9 x 11-inch pan.

Preheat oven to 350°F and line a 9 x 11-inch pan with parchment paper.

Combine quinoa flakes, almonds, salt, cherries or raisins, and flax seeds in a large bowl.

In a small saucepan over low heat, combine coconut oil, honey, maple syrup, and almond or cashew butter, and stir until melted and combined. Pour over quinoa flake mixture and stir to coat.

Press mixture evenly into the bottom of the pan and bake for 25 to 30 minutes or until edges begin to brown.

2 cups quinoa flakes

1 cup sliced almonds

¼ teaspoon salt

1 cup dried cherries or raisins

½ cup flax seeds

¼ cup coconut oil

½ cup honey

¼ cup maple syrup

⅓ cup almond or cashew butter

2 teaspoons vanilla extract

English Tea Squares

Makes one 8 x 8-inch pan.

Preheat oven to 350°F and grease an 8 x 8-inch pan.

In a medium bowl, beat together the butter and sugar until fluffy. Add egg and vanilla and beat until combined.

Add the quinoa flour mix and ground allspice and stir to combine. Fold in the chopped nuts.

Pour half the mixture into the greased pan, spread jam over top, and then add remaining batter in an even layer on top.

Bake about 40 minutes or until top is golden. Remove from oven and cool before cutting into squares.

¾ cup butter, softened

1 cup granulated sugar

1 egg

1 teaspoon vanilla extract

2 cups quinoa flour mix (page 9)

¼ teaspoon ground allspice

1 cup chopped almonds or walnuts

½ cup strawberry jam

Date Sandwich Bars

Makes one 9 x 13-inch pan.

Preheat oven to 400°F and grease a 9 x 13-inch pan.

In a medium saucepan, combine granulated sugar, dates, and water and simmer several minutes until mixture thickens. Remove from heat.

In a mixing bowl, beat together the butter and brown sugar until fluffy.

In a separate bowl, whisk together the quinoa flour mix, baking soda, and salt. Add to the butter and brown sugar mixture and stir to combine. Fold in the quinoa flakes or oats.

Spread half the batter in the greased pan and then spread the date mixture evenly over the top. Add the remaining batter on top and then bake 25 to 30 minutes or until just barely golden.

¼ cup granulated sugar

3 cups pitted and chopped dates

1½ cups water

¾ cup butter, softened

1 cup brown sugar

1¾ cup quinoa flour mix (page 9)

½ teaspoon baking soda

1 teaspoon salt

1½ cups quinoa flakes or oats

Dates are naturally very sweet, so, depending on how sweet you like your bar cookies, you may reduce the brown sugar to as little as ½ cup.

Chocolate Chip Quinoa Cookies

Makes 2 dozen cookies.

Preheat oven to 350°F. Line a baking sheet with parchment paper.

In a large bowl combine almond meal, quinoa flakes, baking soda, and salt and stir until well combined. In a separate bowl, combine eggs, almond butter, applesauce, maple syrup, and vanilla. Mix well and add to the quinoa and almond mixture slowly. Add in chocolate chips.

Using a tablespoon measure, drop cookies onto prepared parchment paper. Flatten slightly with clean fingers. Bake for 12 to 15 minutes, until lightly golden brown. Remove from oven and allow to sit in the pan for 5 minutes. Move to a cooling rack and allow to cool completely.

2 eggs

1 ¼ cups almond meal

1 cup quinoa flakes

¾ teaspoon baking soda

¾ teaspoon salt

½ cup almond butter (peanut or sunflower seed butter would work too)

¼ cup applesauce

¼ cup maple syrup (or other liquid sweetener)

1 teaspoon vanilla extract

¾ cup chocolate chips

This recipe comes from *The Gluten-Free Quintessential Quinoa Cookbook* by Wendy Polisi.

Flourless Chocolate Quinoa Cookies

Makes 1 dozen cookies.

Preheat oven to 350°F. Line a baking sheet with parchment paper.

In a food processor combine almonds and quinoa. Process for 1 minute, or until you have a fine meal. Add baking soda and salt and process until blended.

Heat a small saucepan to medium low and add almond butter and coconut oil. Cook until coconut oil and almond butter are melted, whisking occasionally. Add in applesauce and maple syrup and whisk until heated through. Remove from heat and stir in vanilla and eggs.

Add the warm almond butter mixture to your food processor and process until a dough has formed. Immediately add in the chocolate chips and process until chocolate is melted and blended, stopping to scrape down the sides as necessary.

Roll the dough into small balls and flatten with your fingers. (You could also use a fork.) Bake for 12 to 15 minutes. Allow to cool for 5 minutes in the pan and then transfer to a wire rack to cool completely.

1 cup blanched almonds

1 cup cooked quinoa

¾ teaspoon baking soda

¾ teaspoon salt

⅓ cup almond butter

1 tablespoon coconut oil

¼ cup applesauce

¼ cup maple syrup

1 teaspoon vanilla extract

2 eggs

¾ cup chocolate chips

This recipe comes from *The Gluten-Free Quintessential Quinoa Cookbook* by Wendy Polisi.

Quinoa-Flax Chocolate Chip Cookies

Makes 2 dozen cookies.

Preheat oven to 350°F. Line 2 baking sheets with parchment paper.

In a medium bowl combine flour, quinoa flakes, flaxseed, baking soda, sea salt, and ground cinnamon.

Beat together the butter, applesauce, and sugars on medium high speed until fluffy, about 3 or 4 minutes. Add eggs, one at a time, ensuring the first is fully incorporated before adding the next. Add vanilla and reduce the speed to low. Add in flour mixture and beat until just combined. Stir in chocolate chips.

Drop in teaspoonfuls onto prepared baking sheets. Bake for 9 to 11 minutes. Remove from oven and let the cookies cool for 4 minutes on the baking sheets and then transfer to racks to cool completely.

1 ½ cups quinoa flour mix (page 9)

1 cup quinoa flakes

¼ cup ground flaxseed

1 teaspoon baking soda

1 teaspoon sea salt

½ teaspoon ground cinnamon

1 stick unsalted butter or coconut oil, softened

½ cup applesauce

1 cup coconut sugar (or sugar of choice)

½ cup packed dark brown sugar

2 large eggs

1 ½ teaspoons vanilla extract

1 cup semisweet chocolate chips

This recipe comes from *The Gluten-Free Quintessential Quinoa Cookbook* by Wendy Polisi.

Chocolate Mint Ice Cream Sandwiches

Makes 8 ice cream sandwiches.

Place chocolate chips and coconut oil in the top of a double boiler. (A metal bowl on top of a sauce pan works too.) Melt over medium low until smooth. Remove from heat and allow to cool.

Meanwhile, sift together flour, cocoa powder, baking powder, and salt.

In the bowl of an electric mixer, combine the sugar, applesauce, eggs, mint extract, and vanilla. Beat for 2 ½ minutes on medium speed. Reduce speed to low and add the chocolate. Add flour mixture until just combined. Transfer mixture to a bowl and refrigerate for (at least) 1 hour.

Line 2 baking sheets with parchment paper. Preheat oven to 325°F. Form 16 balls with the cookie dough. Divide the balls between the 2 cookie sheets and flatten slightly. Bake for 15 minutes, rotating the trays halfway through. Let cool for 5 minutes on the pan and then transfer to a wire rack to cool completely.

Allow the ice cream to soften and then spread onto the flat side of one of the cookies. Top with another cookie and wrap with parchment paper, wax paper, or plastic wrap. Freeze for 1 hour, or until firm.

1 cup semisweet chocolate chips

⅓ cup coconut oil

1 cup quinoa flour mix (page 9)

3 tablespoons unsweetened cocoa powder

¾ teaspoon baking powder

¼ teaspoon sea salt

½ cup coconut sugar

¼ cup applesauce

2 eggs, at room temperature

1 teaspoon vanilla extract

½ teaspoon mint extract

Mint chocolate chip or vanilla ice cream

This recipe comes from *The Gluten-Free Quintessential Quinoa Cookbook* by Wendy Polisi.

Chocolate Mint Cookies

Makes 2 dozen cookies.

Preheat oven to 350°F. Line a baking sheet with parchment paper.

Place 2 ounces of chocolate chips and cooked quinoa into a food processor. Process until smooth.

Sift together flour, cocoa powder, palm sugar, baking powder, baking soda, and sea salt. Stir in quinoa mixture.

In a separate bowl combine coconut oil, maple syrup, applesauce, vanilla extract, and mint extract. Whisk until well combined and add to dry ingredients. Stir until just mixed and add in remaining 2 ounces of chocolate chips.

Drop by the tablespoon to prepared baking sheet. Using a wet spoon, flatten the tops of the cookies. Bake for 12 to 18 minutes. Allow to cool for 5 minutes in the pan and then transfer to a rack to cool completely. If desired, top with mint drizzle.

To make mint drizzle combine all ingredients in a small bowl. Add additional milk by the teaspoon until desired texture is reached. Drizzle with a spoon onto cooled cookies. Alternatively, place icing in a small plastic bag and cut the corner to create an icing bag.

4 ounces chocolate chips, divided

½ cup cooked quinoa

1 cup quinoa flour mix (page 9)

¼ cup cocoa powder

¼ cup coconut sugar

1 teaspoon baking powder

½ teaspoon baking soda

¼ teaspoon sea salt

¼ cup coconut oil, melted

⅓ cup maple syrup

¼ cup applesauce

1 teaspoon vanilla extract

½ teaspoon mint extract

MINT DRIZZLE (optional)

½ cup confectioners' sugar

½ tablespoon almond milk

½ teaspoon mint extract

This recipe comes from *The Gluten-Free Quintessential Quinoa Cookbook* by Wendy Polisi.

Cherry and Dark Chocolate Biscotti

Makes about 1 dozen biscotti.

Heat oven to 350°F and grease a baking sheet. In a medium mixing bowl, whisk together the first seven ingredients. In a separate bowl, whisk the two eggs. Place 2 tablespoons of the eggs into a separate dish and set aside. Whisk the olive oil and vanilla into the remaining eggs.

Pour egg, oil, and vanilla mixture into the dry mixture and stir to combine. Fold in the dried cherries and chocolate chips.

Dust a surface with quinoa flour mix and roll out the dough to about ½ inch thickness. Use hands to shape it into a rectangle. Brush with the remaining egg and sprinkle with sliced almonds.

Bake for about 30 minutes, or until top begins to brown. Remove from oven, reduce heat to 250°F, and allow biscotti to cool for about 15 minutes. Transfer biscotti to a cutting board and use a serrated knife to slice into ½-inch wide strips. Place strips cut-side down on baking sheet and return to oven. Bake for 20 minutes, turn biscotti over, and bake another 20 minutes. Transfer biscotti to a wire rack to cool. Store in an airtight container.

¾ cup oat flour

¾ cup quinoa flour mix (page 9)

½ teaspoon xanthan gum

½ cup brown sugar

⅛ teaspoon salt

1½ teaspoons baking powder

½ teaspoon cinnamon

2 eggs

2½ tablespoons olive oil

2 teaspoons vanilla extract

½ cup dried cherries

¼ cup dark chocolate chips

¼ cup sliced almonds

Almond-Orange Biscotti

Makes 2 dozen biscotti.

Preheat oven to 350°F. Line a baking sheet with parchment paper.

In a medium bowl sift together flour, baking powder, and salt. Stir in cooked quinoa.

In a large bowl, beat maple syrup and butter at medium until creamy. Add eggs slowly, scraping down the sides as needed. Add in vanilla, almond extract, and coconut oil.

Reduce mixer to low and add in flour mixture just until combined. Add in almonds and orange zest.

Use floured hands and shape dough into a loaf on parchment-lined baking sheet. Pat the loaf flat on top and smooth with the back of a spoon that had been dipped in cold water. Bake for 35 minutes and remove from oven. Allow to cool on the baking sheet. Reduce oven temperature to 325°F.

Use a serrated knife to cut loaf into ½-inch slices lengthwise. Cut lengths to about 2 ½ to 3 inches long. Place the slices on the baking sheet and bake for 20 to 25 minutes, flipping after 10 minutes. Allow to cool on a wire rack for 1 hour prior to serving.

2 cups quinoa flour mix (page 9)

1 teaspoon baking powder

¼ teaspoon salt

½ cup cooked quinoa

⅔ cup maple syrup

4 tablespoons Earth Balance or unsalted butter, softened slightly

3 room-temperature eggs

1 teaspoon vanilla extract

½ teaspoon almond extract

2 tablespoons melted coconut oil

2 teaspoons orange zest

¾ cup toasted almonds, chopped

This recipe comes from *Gluten-Free Quintessential Desserts* by Wendy Polisi.

Quinoa Applesauce Cookies

Makes 5 dozen cookies.

Preheat oven to 325°F. Grease a cookie sheet.

In a food processor, process sugar and butter until fluffy. Add applesauce, cooked quinoa, and vanilla and process until smooth.

In a large mixing bowl, combine quinoa flour mix, baking soda, salt, cinnamon, and cloves. Add batter from the food processor to your dry mix and stir to combine. Fold in raisins.

Bake for 10 to 12 minutes, or until the edges begin to brown. Remove from oven and allow to cool for a few minutes before transferring cookies to a wire rack.

¾ cup brown sugar or coconut sugar

¾ cup butter, softened

1 cup applesauce

1 cup quinoa, cooked

1 teaspoon vanilla extract

1½ cups quinoa flour mix (page 9)

½ teaspoon baking soda

½ teaspoon salt

1 teaspoon cinnamon

¼ teaspoon cloves

1 cup raisins (optional)

Cakes and Cupcakes

Boston Cream Pie

Makes one 9-inch round cake.

Preheat oven to 375°F. Grease two 9-inch cake pans and dust lightly with gluten-free flour. Beat together the butter and sugar until light and fluffy. Add the vanilla and the eggs, beating after each egg.

In a separate bowl, whisk together the quinoa flour mix, baking powder, and salt. Add to the wet batter alternately with the milk, beating continuously. Divide batter between cake pans and bake for about 25 minutes or until a toothpick inserted into the middle comes out clean. Remove from oven and allow to cool a few minutes before carefully removing from pans and transferring to cooling racks.

To make the filling, in a small bowl, mix together the quinoa flour mix, salt, water, egg, and butter. In a medium saucepan, bring the milk to a slow boil. Add the flour mixture and stir until the filling thickens to a pudding consistency (several minutes). Remove from heat and allow to cool. Add vanilla and mix.

Assemble the cake before making the glaze. Place first cake layer on a cake plate, spread cream filling over the top, and place second cake layer on top.

To make the glaze, place chocolate and heavy cream in a small saucepan and heat slowly, stirring constantly until melted. Pour over top of the cake and use a spatula or wide knife to spread as needed.

CAKE

½ cup butter, softened

1½ cups granulated sugar

1 teaspoon vanilla extract

2 eggs

2¼ cup quinoa flour mix (page 9)

2½ teaspoons baking powder

1 teaspoon salt

1 cup milk

CREAM FILLING

1 cup granulated sugar

2 tablespoons quinoa flour mix (page 9)

¼ teaspoon salt

2 tablespoons cold water

1 egg

1 tablespoon butter

1 cup milk

1 teaspoon vanilla extract

CHOCOLATE GLAZE

4 ounces quality chocolate

½ cup heavy cream

Cakes and Cupcakes

Gingerbread Pumpkin Cupcakes with Spiced Cream

Makes 1 dozen cupcakes.

Preheat oven to 350°F. Grease a muffin tin and dust with gluten-free flour, or line with cupcake liners.

In a large mixing bowl, whisk together the flour, baking powder, ginger, cinnamon, salt, and brown sugar. In a separate bowl, whisk together the oil, eggs, vanilla, and pumpkin. Add the flour mixture to the wet mixture and stir to combine.

Fill muffin cups about ¾ full and bake for about 15 minutes, or until a toothpick inserted in the center of a cupcake comes out clean. Remove from oven and allow to cool completely.

While cupcakes are cooling, make the spiced cream. In a medium bowl, beat the heavy cream until it becomes light and fluffy. Add the honey and vanilla and beat until desired consistency is reached. It should be fairly stiff to hold its shape on the cupcakes. Scoop cream into a pastry bag fitted with a wide round tip. Arrange cupcakes on serving tray. Just before serving, swirl cream on top of each cupcake. Sprinkle with ground cinnamon and serve immediately.

CUPCAKES

2 cups quinoa flour mix (page 9)

2 teaspoons baking powder

2 teaspoons ground ginger

1 teaspoon ground cinnamon

¼ teaspoon salt

1 cup dark brown sugar

½ cup vegetable oil

2 eggs

2 teaspoons vanilla extract

1 cup pumpkin puree

SPICED CREAM

1 cup heavy cream

1 tablespoon honey

½ teaspoon vanilla

Ground cinnamon

Chocolate Bundt Cake with Sour Cream Glaze

Makes 1 bundt cake.

Preheat oven to 375°F. Brew coffee. Grease the bundt pan and generously sift cocoa powder over it to prevent the cake from sticking after it's baked.

In a large bowl, whisk together the brewed coffee, buttermilk, butter, and cocoa powder. Add the sugar and whisk until dissolved. Allow to cool.

In a separate bowl, whisk together the flour, baking soda, and salt. Allow butter mixture to cool if it's still hot from the brewed coffee. Whisk in the egg and vanilla and mix until combined.

Pour the mixture into the bundt pan and bake 20 to 25 minutes, or until a toothpick inserted into one comes out clean. Remove from oven and allow to cool completely before removing from pan.

Meanwhile, prepare the glaze. In a double boiler, melt the chocolate pieces, stirring constantly. Add the butter and continue stirring until incorporated. Gradually add the confectioners' sugar, and then the sour cream. Whisk until glossy.

Carefully remove the bundt cake from the pan and place on large cutting board or other work surface. Drizzle the glaze over the cake and then allow to sit until glaze sets. Garnish as desired.

CAKE

½ cup brewed coffee

½ cup buttermilk (or ½ cup milk mixed with ½ teaspoon vinegar)

½ cup unsalted butter, melted

½ cup cocoa powder, plus more for dusting the pan

1 cup granulated sugar

1 cup quinoa flour mix (page 9)

¾ teaspoon baking soda

¼ teaspoon salt

1 egg

½ teaspoon vanilla extract

SOUR CREAM GLAZE

6 ounces bittersweet chocolate, chopped

¾ cup unsalted butter

1 cup confectioners' sugar

½ cup sour cream or Greek-style yogurt

GARNISH (optional)

Fresh berries, crushed nuts, or sifted confectioners' sugar

Cranberry Pound Cake with Lemon Glaze

Makes 1 loaf.

Preheat oven to 350°F. Grease a loaf pan and generously dust with confectioners' sugar to prevent the cake from sticking after it's baked.

In a medium mixing bowl, beat together the butter and brown sugar. Add the eggs, one at a time, while beating, and then add the vanilla.

In a separate bowl, whisk together the flour, baking powder, and salt. Add the flour mixture to the wet mixture, stirring to combine. Fold in the cranberries and then pour into loaf pan. Bake 30 minutes, or until a toothpick inserted into the center comes out clean. Remove from oven and allow to cool completely before removing from pan.

Meanwhile, prepare the glaze. Mix together confectioners' sugar and milk until smooth. Add lemon juice and whisk.

Carefully remove the cake from the pan and place on large cutting board or other work surface. Drizzle the glaze over the cake and then allow to sit until glaze sets.

CAKE

Confectioners' sugar (for dusting pan)

1 cup butter, unsalted

1 1/4 cups brown sugar

3 eggs

1 teaspoon vanilla extract

1 1/2 cups quinoa flour mix (page 9)

1 1/2 teaspoons baking powder

1/2 teaspoon salt

2 cups cranberries

LEMON GLAZE

2 cups confectioners' sugar

2 tablespoons milk

2 teaspoons lemon juice

Apple Raspberry Quinoa Cake

Makes one 9-inch round cake.

Preheat oven to 350°F and grease a 9-inch cake pan. Beat together the butter and sugar until fluffy. Add applesauce and egg and beat until well mixed. Add cooked quinoa and stir.

In a separate bowl, combine quinoa flour mix and baking powder. Add to wet mixture and stir. Fold in apple chunks and raspberries.

Bake for about 50 minutes, or until a toothpick inserted into the center comes out fairly clean.

4 tablespoons butter, softened

¾ cup brown sugar or honey

½ cup applesauce

1 egg, lightly beaten

1 cup cooked quinoa

1 cup quinoa flour mix (page 9)

1½ teaspoons baking powder

2 apples, peeled and cut into small chunks

1 cup fresh or thawed raspberries

If you use honey instead of sugar in this recipe, reduce the oven temperature to 325°F and bake for slightly longer. Honey makes baked goods brown more quickly than sugar, and you don't want a dark brown cake with a raw center.

Rich Chocolate Honey Cake

Makes 1 double-layer cake.

Preheat oven to 325°F. Grease two 9-inch cake pans.

Pour the buttermilk and honey into a food processor and blend for about a minute. This will add air to the mixture, resulting in a lighter cake. Add the cooked quinoa and eggs and process until smooth. Add vanilla, butter, and applesauce, and blend until fully combined. Add remaining ingredients and pulse just until mixed.

Pour into two cake pans and bake for about 45 minutes or until a toothpick inserted into the center comes out relatively clean. Remove from oven and allow to cool before removing from pans.

To make the whipped topping, beat heavy cream with the vanilla and honey until light and fluffy. Spread over first cake, place second cake on top, and then spread over top. Serve immediately.

CAKE

¼ cup buttermilk

¾ cup honey

2 cups cooked quinoa, cooled

4 eggs

1 teaspoon vanilla extract

½ cup butter, softened

½ cup applesauce

1 cup unsweetened cocoa powder

1 teaspoon baking soda

1½ teaspoons baking powder

½ teaspoon salt

TOPPING

1 pint heavy cream

1 teaspoon vanilla

1 teaspoon honey

Rich Chocolate Cake with Chocolate Mascarpone Frosting

Makes 1 double-layer cake.

Preheat oven to 325°F. Grease two 9-inch cake pans and dust with gluten-free flour.

Pour the milk, eggs, and vanilla in a food processor and blend for about a minute. Add the cooked quinoa and applesauce and process until smooth. Add coconut oil or butter and sugar and blend until fully combined. Add remaining ingredients and pulse just until mixed.

Pour into two cake pans and bake for about 45 minutes or until a toothpick inserted into the center comes out relatively clean. Remove from oven and allow to cool before removing from pans.

To make the frosting, beat heavy cream with the honey until light and fluffy. Add mascarpone and cocoa powder and beat until frosting consistency. Spread over first cake, place second cake on top, and then spread over top and sides. Sprinkle coconut flakes over the top and gently press into sides.

CAKE

⅓ cup milk (dairy, almond, coconut, or soy)

4 eggs

1 teaspoon vanilla extract

2 cups cooked quinoa, cooled

½ cup applesauce

½ cup coconut oil or butter

1 cup sugar

1½ teaspoons baking powder

½ teaspoon baking soda

½ teaspoon salt

FROSTING

1 pint heavy cream

8 ounces mascarpone cheese

3 tablespoons cocoa powder

1 teaspoon honey

2 cups coconut flakes, for garnish

Pumpkin Cheesecake with a Quinoa Maple Crust

Makes one 9-inch round cheesecake.

Preheat oven to 375°F.

To make the crust, mix together all crust ingredients. Grease a 9-inch pie plate or springform pan, and then press the mixture into the bottom of the plate and up the sides. Bake for 10 minutes and then remove from oven.

To make the filling, beat the cream cheese until fluffy. Add the brown sugar, pumpkin, sour cream, vanilla, cinnamon, ginger, and salt, and beat until well combined. Add eggs one at a time, beating after each addition.

Pour filling into the crust and bake for about 45 minutes, or until filling is set. If you find that the crust is getting too dark while the cheesecake is baking, wrap the edges in tinfoil, being careful not to burn your fingers on the pie plate. Remove from oven.

Mix together topping ingredients in a medium bowl and then spread evenly over the top of the cheesecake. Bake for another 5 minutes and then remove from oven.

Allow to cool on a wire rack and then refrigerate several hours or overnight.

CRUST

2 cups cooked quinoa
½ cup brown rice flour
1 egg
¼ cup butter or coconut oil, melted
4 tablespoons maple syrup
½ teaspoon ground cinnamon
½ teaspoon ground ginger

FILLING

1½ (8-ounce) packages cream cheese, softened
½ cup light brown sugar
1 cup pumpkin puree
¾ cup sour cream
1 teaspoon vanilla extract
½ teaspoon ground cinnamon
½ teaspoon ground ginger
¼ teaspoon salt
2 eggs

TOPPING

¾ cup sour cream
¼ cup granulated sugar
1 tablespoon maple syrup
1 teaspoon vanilla extract

Key Lime Pie with a Quinoa Honey Crust

Makes one 9-inch pie.

Preheat oven to 375°F.

To make the crust, mix together all crust ingredients. Grease a 9-inch pie plate or springform pan, and then press the mixture into the bottom of the plate and up the sides. Bake for about 20 minutes and then remove from oven.

Reduce oven temperature to 325°F. To make the filling, beat together the eggs, sweetened condensed milk, and lime juice. Pour into crust and bake for about 15 minutes. Remove from oven and chill in the refrigerator for at least 2 hours before serving.

CRUST

2 cups cooked quinoa

½ cup brown rice flour

1 egg

¼ cup butter or coconut oil

4 tablespoons honey

½ teaspoon ground cinnamon

½ teaspoon ground ginger

FILLING

3 eggs

2 (14-ounce) cans sweetened condensed milk

¾ cup fresh-squeezed lime juice

Key lime pie should really be made with key limes, but since they're not readily available to many of us for most of the year, any fresh lime juice will do.

Peanut Butter Pie with a Raspberry Quinoa Crust

Makes one 9-inch pie.

Preheat oven to 375°F.

To make the crust, mix together all crust ingredients. Grease a 9-inch pie plate or springform pan, and then press the mixture into the bottom of the plate and up the sides. Bake for about 20 minutes and then remove from oven and allow to cool completely. Spread the raspberry jam over the bottom of the shell.

To make the filling, in a large bowl, beat together the cream cheese, sugar, and peanut butter until fluffy. In a separate bowl, whip the cream with the vanilla until stiff peaks form.

Use a big spoon or a rubber spatula to fold the whipped cream into the other batter. Pour the mixture into the baked pie shell and chill for at least 4 hours.

CRUST

2 cups cooked quinoa

½ cup brown rice flour

1 egg

¼ cup butter or coconut oil

4 tablespoons maple syrup

½ teaspoon ground cinnamon

½ teaspoon ground ginger

1 cup raspberry jam

FILLING

1 (8-ounce) package cream cheese

½ cup granulated sugar

1 cup smooth peanut butter

1 cup heavy whipping cream

1 teaspoon vanilla extract

Blueberry-Peach Upside Down Cake

Makes one 9-inch cake.

Preheat oven to 350°F and grease a 9-inch round cake pan. Fresh fruit should be washed and dried before using; frozen fruit should be used frozen (don't thaw).

For the Topping: Place the cake pan over a burner and turn the heat to low. Add 3 tablespoons butter and allow to melt. Add sugar and stir until dissolved. Turn off the burner. Arrange the berries and peach slices on the bottom of the cake pan, in the sugar-butter syrup.

For the Cake: In a food processor, cream together the butter or coconut oil and brown sugar or coconut sugar. Add quinoa and process until smooth. Add yogurt, applesauce, vanilla, and eggs, and process another 30 seconds or until fully combined. In a separate large bowl, combine the quinoa flour mix, baking powder, baking soda, salt, and ginger. Pour wet mixture from the food processor into the dry mixture and stir to combine.

Pour batter over top of the fruit and bake for 30 to 40 minutes, or until the top is golden and a toothpick inserted into the center comes out clean. Remove from oven. While the cake is still hot, place a plate or baking sheet over top of the cake and, using oven mitts, flip it over. You may need to run a knife around the edge of the pan to loosen the sides.

TOPPING

3 tablespoons butter or coconut oil

1/4 cup light brown or coconut sugar

1 1/2 cups fresh or frozen blueberries

1 cup fresh or frozen peach slices (peeled)

CAKE

4 tablespoons butter or coconut oil, melted

1/3 cup light brown sugar or coconut sugar

1 cup cooked quinoa

1/2 cup plain yogurt

1/4 cup unsweetened applesauce

2 teaspoons pure vanilla extract

2 eggs

3/4 cup quinoa flour mix (page 9)

2 teaspoons baking powder

1/2 teaspoon baking soda

1/2 teaspoon salt

1/2 teaspoon ginger

Cinnamon Coffee Cake

Makes one 9-inch cake.

Preheat oven to 350°F and grease a 9-inch round cake pan.

For the Cake: In a food processor, cream together the butter or coconut oil and brown sugar or coconut sugar. Add quinoa and process until smooth. Add yogurt, applesauce, vanilla, and eggs, and process another 30 seconds or so until fully combined.

In a separate large bowl, combine the quinoa flour mix, baking powder, baking soda, salt, and ginger. Pour wet mixture from the food processor into the dry mixture and stir to combine. Pour into prepared pan.

For the Topping: Combine oats, cooked quinoa, almonds, sugar, and butter and mix. Sprinkle evenly over cake.

Bake about 30 minutes, or until topping is gold and a toothpick inserted into the center comes out clean.

CAKE

4 tablespoons butter or coconut oil, melted

1/3 cup light brown sugar or coconut sugar

1 cup cooked quinoa

1/2 cup plain yogurt

1/4 cup unsweetened applesauce

2 teaspoons pure vanilla extract

2 eggs

3/4 cup quinoa flour mix (page 9)

2 teaspoons baking powder

1/2 teaspoon baking soda

1/2 teaspoon salt

1/2 teaspoon ginger

CRUMB TOPPING

3/4 cup gluten-free oats

3/4 cup cooked quinoa

1/2 cup sliced almonds

3/4 cup brown sugar or coconut sugar

1 stick (1/2 cup) butter, softened

Ginger Lemon Coffee Cake

Makes one 9-inch cake.

Preheat oven to 350°F and grease a 9-inch round cake pan.

For the Cake: In a food processor, cream together the butter or coconut oil and brown sugar or coconut sugar. Add quinoa and process until smooth. Add yogurt, applesauce, lemon juice, lemon zest, and eggs, and process another 30 seconds or so until fully combined.

In a separate large bowl, combine the quinoa flour mix, baking powder, baking soda, salt, and ginger. Pour wet mixture from the food processor into the dry mixture and stir to combine.

For the Topping: Combine oats, cooked quinoa, sugar, and butter and mix. Stir in crystallized ginger. Sprinkle topping evenly over cake.

Bake about 30 minutes, or until topping is gold and a toothpick inserted into the center comes out clean.

CAKE

4 tablespoons butter or coconut oil, melted

⅓ cup light brown sugar or coconut sugar

1 cup cooked quinoa

½ cup plain yogurt

¼ cup unsweetened applesauce

2 teaspoons lemon juice

1 teaspoon lemon zest

2 eggs

¾ cup quinoa flour mix (page 9)

2 teaspoons baking powder

½ teaspoon baking soda

½ teaspoon salt

1 teaspoon ginger

CRUMB TOPPING

¾ cup gluten-free oats

¾ cup cooked quinoa

¾ cup brown sugar or coconut sugar

1 stick (½ cup) butter, softened

¼ cup crystallized ginger, cut into small pieces

Pear and Pecan Coffee Cake

Makes one 9-inch cake.

Preheat oven to 350°F and grease a 9-inch round cake pan.

For the Cake: In a food processor, cream together the butter or coconut oil and brown sugar or coconut sugar. Add quinoa and process until smooth. Add yogurt, applesauce, and eggs, and process another 30 seconds or so until fully combined.

In a separate large bowl, combine the quinoa flour mix, baking powder, baking soda, salt, and cinnamon. Pour wet mixture from the food processor into the dry mixture and stir to combine. Add chopped pears and stir.

For the Topping: Combine oats, cooked quinoa, sugar, and butter and mix. Stir in chopped pecans. Sprinkle evenly over cake.

Bake about 30 minutes, or until topping is gold and a toothpick inserted into the center comes out clean.

CAKE

4 tablespoons butter or coconut oil, melted
1/3 cup light brown sugar or coconut sugar
1 cup cooked quinoa
1/2 cup plain yogurt
1/4 cup unsweetened applesauce
2 eggs
3/4 cup quinoa flour mix (page 9)
2 teaspoons baking powder
1/2 teaspoon baking soda
1/2 teaspoon salt
1 teaspoon ground cinnamon
2 pears, peeled, seeded, and chopped

CRUMB TOPPING

3/4 cup gluten-free oats
3/4 cup cooked quinoa
3/4 cup brown sugar or coconut sugar
1 stick (1/2 cup) butter, softened
1/2 cup chopped pecans

Cherry Almond Coffee Cake

Makes one 9-inch cake.

Preheat oven to 350°F and grease a 9-inch round cake pan.

For the Cake: In a food processor, cream together the butter or coconut oil and brown sugar or coconut sugar. Add quinoa and process until smooth. Add yogurt, applesauce, eggs, and almond flavoring, and process another 30 seconds or so until fully combined.

In a separate large bowl, combine the quinoa flour mix, baking powder, baking soda, and salt. Pour wet mixture from the food processor into the dry mixture and stir to combine. Add chopped cherries and stir.

For the Topping: Combine oats, cooked quinoa, sugar, and butter and mix. Stir in chopped almonds. Sprinkle evenly over cake.

Bake about 30 minutes, or until topping is gold and a toothpick inserted into the center comes out clean.

CAKE

4 tablespoons butter or coconut oil, melted
$^1/_3$ cup light brown sugar or coconut sugar
1 cup cooked quinoa
$^1/_2$ cup plain yogurt
$^1/_4$ cup unsweetened applesauce
2 eggs
1 teaspoon almond flavoring
$^3/_4$ cup quinoa flour mix (page 9)
2 teaspoons baking powder
$^1/_2$ teaspoon baking soda
$^1/_2$ teaspoon salt
1 cup pitted, chopped cherries

CRUMB TOPPING

$^3/_4$ cup gluten-free oats
$^3/_4$ cup cooked quinoa
$^3/_4$ cup brown sugar or coconut sugar
1 stick ($^1/_2$ cup) butter, softened
$^1/_2$ cup chopped almonds

Tea Breads, Muffins, and Scones

Quinoa Oat Pumpkin Muffins

Makes 1 dozen muffins.

Preheat oven to 375°F. Grease a 12-cup muffin tin or line with cupcake liners. Whisk together all the dry ingredients. In a separate bowl, whisk together the pumpkin, oil, milk, vanilla, and eggs and add to the dry ingredients, mixing until incorporated.

Add the chocolate chips, raisins, cranberries, or chopped apple and stir just until evenly distributed. Fill muffin tins nearly full and bake for about 20 minutes or until a toothpick inserted into the center of a muffin comes out fairly clean.

1½ cups quinoa flour mix (page 9)

1½ cups gluten-free, old-fashioned oats

½ cup brown sugar or ⅓ cup maple syrup or honey

1 teaspoon baking powder

½ teaspoon baking soda

½ teaspoon salt

1 teaspoon cinnamon

1 teaspoon ground ginger

1½ cups pumpkin puree

3 tablespoons olive oil or melted coconut oil

¼ cup milk (dairy, almond, coconut, or soy)

2 teaspoons vanilla extract

2 eggs, lightly beaten

½ cup dark chocolate chips, raisins, cranberries, or peeled, chopped apple (optional)

I like the flavor of oats in these muffins, but you could certainly replace the oats with quinoa flakes if you wish!

Lemon Poppy Seed Muffins

Makes 1 dozen muffins.

Preheat oven to 400°F and grease a 12-cup muffin tin.

In a medium bowl, stir together all the dry ingredients.

In a separate bowl, mix together the melted butter or coconut oil, eggs, milk, and lemon juice. Add the dry ingredients to the wet and mix just until combined. Add poppy seeds and stir to distribute.

Pour batter into prepared pan and bake for about 20 minutes, or until a toothpick inserted into the center of a muffin comes out clean.

2 cups quinoa flour mix
   (page 9)
½ teaspoon xanthan gum
½ teaspoon salt
1 tablespoon baking powder
½ cup brown sugar
4 tablespoons unsalted butter or
   coconut oil, melted
2 large eggs
1 cup milk
1 teaspoon lemon juice
2 tablespoons poppy seeds

Chocolate Chip Muffins

Makes 1 dozen muffins.

Preheat oven to 400°F and grease a 12-cup muffin tin.

In a medium bowl, stir together all the dry ingredients.

In a separate bowl, mix together the melted butter or coconut oil, eggs, and milk. Add the dry ingredients to the wet and mix just until combined. Add chocolate chips and stir to distribute.

Pour batter into prepared pan and bake for about 20 minutes, or until a toothpick inserted into the center of a muffin comes out clean.

2 cups quinoa flour mix (page 9)

½ teaspoon xanthan gum

½ teaspoon salt

1 tablespoon baking powder

½ cup brown sugar

4 tablespoons unsalted butter or coconut oil, melted

2 large eggs

1 cup milk

¾ cup semisweet chocolate chips

Cinnamon Carrot Muffins

Makes 9 muffins.

Preheat oven to 350°F. Line a muffin tin with 9 paper cups.

In a large bowl combine quinoa flour mix, cooked quinoa, coconut palm sugar, cinnamon, baking powder, baking soda and sea salt.

Combine milk and lemon juice in a small bowl. Set aside to curdle.

In a medium bowl combine milk mixture, eggs, and applesauce. Whisk until well combined. Add coconut oil and vanilla extract. Stir until combined and then add wet mixture to the dry mixture.

Stir in carrots until just combined and spoon batter into cups. Bake for 22 to 28 minutes, until a toothpick comes out clean.

Cool in pan for 10 minutes and then transfer to a wire rack to continue cooling. Top with cinnamon drizzle if desired.

For the drizzle: Combine all ingredients in a small bowl. Add additional milk until desired texture is achieved.

1 cup quinoa flour mix (page 9)

½ cup cooked quinoa

½ cup coconut palm sugar

1 teaspoon ground cinnamon

2 teaspoons baking powder

1 teaspoon baking soda

¼ teaspoon sea salt

⅓ cup dairy or soy milk

1 teaspoon lemon juice

2 room-temperature eggs

¼ cup applesauce

⅓ cup coconut oil, melted

1 teaspoon vanilla extract

2 cups shredded carrots

CINNAMON DRIZZLE (optional)

½ cup powdered sugar

½ teaspoon cinnamon

½ tablespoon almond milk or milk of choice

This recipe comes from *The Gluten-Free Quintessential Quinoa Cookbook* by Wendy Polisi.

Sweet Potato Scones

Makes 1 dozen scones.

Preheat oven to 425°F and grease a baking sheet. Heat a pan of water to boiling. Peel and chop the sweet potato into 1-inch chunks. Boil for about 6 minutes or until soft when pricked with a fork. Drain, mash, and place in refrigerator to chill.

Whisk together flours, brown sugar, baking powder, xanthan gum, salt, and cinnamon. Cut the butter or oil into the flour mixture and use your fingers to incorporate until the mixture resembles coarse crumbs.

In a small bowl, whisk together the egg, milk, and vanilla. Pour into the flour mixture, add mashed sweet potato, and stir to combine. Turn the dough onto a lightly floured surface, divide into two balls, and knead each 7 or 8 times. Place dough balls on cookie sheet and flatten each into circles that are about ¾-inch thick. Slice into sixths but don't separate the wedges.

Bake for about 20 minutes or until tops and edges begin to brown. Dough will still be moist in the center. Remove from oven, use a spatula to separate the wedges, and cool on racks. Store in an airtight container in the refrigerator or freezer.

1 medium sweet potato
   (about 1 cup mashed)
1½ cups quinoa flour mix (page 9)
¾ cup oat flour
¼ cup brown sugar
2 teaspoons baking powder
½ teaspoon xanthan gum
¼ teaspoon salt
1 teaspoon cinnamon
6 tablespoons butter or coconut oil, cold
1 egg
4 tablespoons cold milk
1 teaspoon vanilla

Keeping all the ingredients cold while preparing the dough will result in flakier scones. Scones are best served warm and are delicious with jam.

Cranberry Quinoa Scones

Makes 8 scones.

Preheat oven to 400°F. Line a baking sheet with parchment paper.

In a small bowl, combine almond milk and lemon juice. Set aside to curdle.

In a large bowl sift together brown rice flour, sorghum flour, quinoa flour, potato starch, tapioca starch, xanthan gum, sugar, baking powder, baking soda, and salt. Stir in orange peel. Using fingers or a pastry cutter, mix in butter until you have a coarse meal. Stir in cranberries.

Mix in milk mixture, ¼ cup at a time, mixing with a fork as you go. Place mixture on a sheet of parchment paper and knead briefly. Form into a round, about an inch thick. Cut into 8 pieces.

Transfer pieces to parchment-lined baking sheet. Bake for about 25 minutes. Remove from oven and allow to sit on the baking sheet for another 10 minutes. Serve warm.

1 cup chilled almond milk (or milk of choice)

1 tablespoon lemon juice

1 cup extra-fine brown rice flour

¾ cup sorghum flour

½ cup quinoa flour, roasted (page 8)

½ cup potato starch

¼ cup tapioca starch

1½ teaspoons xanthan gum

⅓ cup coconut palm sugar

3 teaspoons baking powder

½ teaspoon baking soda

1¼ teaspoons kosher salt

1 tablespoon grated orange peel

¾ cup chilled Earth Balance or unsalted butter

¾ cup dried cranberries

This recipe comes from *The Gluten-Free Quintessential Quinoa Cookbook* by Wendy Polisi.

Cherry Clafoutis

Makes 1 dozen clafoutis.

Preheat oven to 325°F. Grease 12 muffin cups. In a large mixing bowl, beat together eggs, sugar, lemon zest, and vanilla. Add milk and beat another 30 seconds or so. Stir in the flour and salt.

Fill each muffin cup about ⅔ of the way, place 3 or 4 cherry halves on top of the batter in each cup, and bake for 20 to 25 minutes, or until a toothpick inserted in the middle of one comes out clean.

Just before serving, dust with confectioners' sugar.

4 eggs

¾ cup sugar

2 teaspoons lemon zest

1 teaspoon vanilla

1 cup milk (dairy, coconut, soy, or almond)

¾ cup quinoa flour mix (page 9)

¼ teaspoon salt

1 cup halved and pitted cherries

Confectioners' sugar, for dusting

Dainty and delicious, clafoutis are perfect with a cup of afternoon tea!

Moist Zucchini Quick Bread

Makes 1 loaf.

Preheat oven to 375°F and grease a loaf pan.

In a large bowl bowl, mix together the quinoa flour mix, baking soda, baking powder, and salt. In a food processor, combine quinoa, sugar, eggs, butter or coconut oil, and vanilla. Process until smooth.

Pour into the large bowl containing the dry ingredients and stir to mix. Fold in zucchini and then pour batter into greased loaf pan.

Bake for about 45 minutes, or until a toothpick inserted into the center comes out relatively clean.

1 cup quinoa flour mix (page 9)

½ teaspoon baking soda

¼ teaspoon baking powder

½ teaspoon salt

1 cup cooked quinoa, cooled

1 cup sugar

2 eggs

3 tablespoons butter or coconut oil, melted

1 teaspoon vanilla extract

2 cups shredded zucchini

Quinoa Banana Bread

Makes 1 loaf.

Preheat oven to 375°F and grease a loaf pan.

In a large bowl, mix together the quinoa flour mix, baking soda, and salt. In a food processor, combine quinoa, sugar, bananas, egg, butter or coconut oil, and vanilla. Process until smooth.

Pour into the large bowl containing the dry ingredients and stir to mix. Fold in chocolate chips and then pour batter into greased loaf pan.

Bake for about 45 minutes, or until a toothpick inserted into the center comes out relatively clean.

1 cup quinoa flour mix (page 9)
½ teaspoon baking soda
½ teaspoon salt
1 cup cooked quinoa, cooled
½ cup sugar
2 very ripe bananas
2 eggs
3 tablespoons butter or coconut oil, melted
1 teaspoon vanilla extract
¾ cup chocolate chips

Quinoa and Almond Flour Banana Bread

Makes 1 loaf.

Preheat oven to 350°F and grease a loaf pan.

In a large mixing bowl, whisk together all dry ingredients. In a separate bowl, mix together the wet ingredients. Fold the wet ingredients into the dry and mix to incorporate. Mix in chocolate chips, raisins, or walnuts if using.

Pour into the loaf pan and bake 35 to 40 minutes or until a toothpick inserted into the center comes out fairly clean. Allow to cool until pan can be handled and then remove from pan and continue cooling on a wire rack.

1½ cups quinoa flour mix (page 9)
1½ cups almond flour
1 teaspoon baking soda
½ teaspoon baking powder
½ teaspoon salt
3 eggs
2 to 3 very ripe bananas, mashed
⅓ cup brown sugar, honey, or maple syrup
¼ cup butter or coconut oil, softened
1 teaspoon vanilla extract
1 cup chocolate chips, raisins, or walnuts (optional)

Pumpkin Pancakes

Makes 6 servings.

Coat a griddle or skillet with cooking spray and heat to medium low or 350 to 375°F.

Sift together flour blend, baking powder, baking soda, cinnamon, ginger, and sea salt.

In a separate bowl combine almond milk, pumpkin puree, lemon juice, eggs, sweetener, melted coconut oil, and vanilla extract.

Combine wet ingredients with the flour mixture and stir until combined. Add quinoa and mix well. Add more milk one tablespoon at a time if a thinner pancake is desired.

Drop batter onto griddle using ¼-cup measure. Cook until the bottom is golden brown and the air bubbles start to pop. Flip and cook 3 to 5 minutes longer.

2 cups quinoa flour mix
 (see page 9)
2 teaspoons baking powder
1 teaspoon baking soda
1 teaspoon cinnamon
½ teaspoon ground ginger
¾ teaspoon sea salt
1¾ cups milk or almond milk
¾ cup pumpkin puree
2 teaspoons lemon juice
2 eggs
1 tablespoon coconut nectar, maple
 syrup or agave
1 tablespoon melted
 coconut oil
1 teaspoon vanilla extract
1 cup cooked quinoa

This recipe comes from *The Gluten-Free Quintessential Quinoa Cookbook* by Wendy Polisi.

Pies, Tarts, Crisps, and Crumbles

Cherry Mascarpone Tartlets

Makes about 2 dozen tartlets.

Preheat oven to 350°F. Generously grease a mini tart tin with cooking spray or butter. In a large mixing bowl, whisk together the flour, almond meal, xanthan gum, sugar, and salt. Add the melted butter, vanilla, and milk, and mix. Use your hands to knead the dough until it hangs together and becomes smooth.

Take a small chunk of dough, roll it into a ball between your palms, and place it in one of the tart cups. Use a pestle (from a mortar and pestle) to press the dough down so that it spreads up the sides of the cup. Repeat until all cups are filled.

Place mini tart tin in the oven and bake for about 10 minutes or until the shells are slightly golden. Remove from oven, press the dough down again if it has puffed up, and allow to cool.

In a medium bowl, mix together mascarpone cheese, cherries, almond extract, and honey. Fill each tartlet shell with the mixture and garnish with the toasted almonds or pistachios.

SHELLS

1 cup quinoa flour mix (page 9)
½ cup almond meal
½ teaspoon xanthan gum
¼ cup sugar
¼ teaspoon salt
4 tablespoons butter, melted
1 teaspoon vanilla
3 tablespoons milk

FILLING

1 cup mascarpone cheese
½ cup pitted cherries, crushed into small pieces
1 teaspoon almond extract
1 tablespoon honey
1 cup toasted almonds, chopped, or pistachios

Raspberry Peach Cobbler

Makes 8 to 10 servings.

Preheat oven to 350°F.

In a large bowl, mix together peach slices, raspberries, and cornstarch. Divide between 8 to 10 ramekins.

In a medium mixing bowl, combine oats, flour, brown sugar, cinnamon, and nutmeg. Mix the butter in, using two forks, a pastry cutter, or your fingers to incorporate.

Place ramekins on a cookie sheet and divide topping between them. Bake for 35 to 40 minutes, or until topping is golden and bubbly. Cool before serving so that ramekins don't burn your fingers.

5 medium peaches, peeled and sliced

2 cups fresh or frozen raspberries

1 tablespoon cornstarch

¾ cup gluten-free oats

¾ cup quinoa flour mix (page 9)

1 cup brown sugar

1 teaspoon cinnamon

½ teaspoon nutmeg

1 stick (½ cup) butter, cut into pieces

Rather than baking in ramekins, you can bake in a 2-quart casserole dish or a deep pie plate and then scoop into tea cups to serve, as shown here.

Rustic Plum Galettes

Makes about 6 small galettes.

In a food processor, combine flour, almond flour, xanthan gum, salt, and sugar and pulse to mix. Add the coconut oil and pulse until coarse crumbs form. Add cider and 4 tablespoons water, pulse, and then add 1 tablespoon water at a time until dough hangs together. Place a large piece of parchment paper on a flat work surface, form dough into a ball, and place the ball on top of the paper. Cover with another large piece of parchment paper and roll out to about ⅛ inch thick. Refrigerate for about 20 minutes.

Mix together the maple syrup or honey, ground almonds, cornstarch, and preserves in a small mixing bowl. When the dough is chilled, preheat oven to 375°F. Cut the dough into circles about 4 inches in diameter and arrange on a baking sheet. Gather dough scraps and repeat.

Spread the dough rounds with the filling mixture, leaving a 1-inch border. Dot with coconut oil, and then arrange a few plum slices on each one. Fold up the pastry edges, pressing lightly to adhere as necessary.

Bake for 40 to 45 minutes, or until pastry is golden. Remove from oven and cool on wire racks.

Make sure the coconut oil is soft but not liquid when you use it. If it's too hard, heat it briefly until it softens up. If it's too liquidy, chill it before use.

PASTRY

1½ cups quinoa flour mix (page 9)
½ cup almond flour
2 teaspoons xanthan gum
¼ teaspoon salt
2 tablespoons sugar
8 tablespoons coconut oil, soft but not liquid
2 teaspoons cider vinegar
6 to 8 tablespoons ice water

PLUM FILLING

¼ cup maple syrup or honey
3 tablespoons ground almonds
1 tablespoon cornstarch
½ cup plum, apricot, or raspberry preserves
2 tablespoons coconut oil
2 pounds fresh plums, pitted and sliced into thin wedges

Classic Whoopie Pies

Makes about 8 whoopie pies.

Preheat oven to 350°F with rack in middle. Line two baking sheets with parchment paper or silicone baking mats and set aside.

Sift cocoa powder, flour, baking powder, baking soda, and salt into a large bowl. In a separate bowl, beat together butter and sugar until fluffy. Add egg and vanilla and mix until all are combined. Add half the dry mixture to the butter mixture and mix well. Slowly add in buttermilk and continue mixing. When mixture is consistent, add remaining dry mixture and mix until smooth.

Scoop heaping tablespoons of batter onto the prepared pans. Allow about 2 inches of space between each as cakes will spread as they bake.

Bake on center rack for 15 to 18 minutes, until a toothpick inserted comes out clean and the cakes spring back when touched. Remove from oven and immediately transfer cakes and parchment paper onto a cooling rack to cool completely.

To prepare the filling, beat together the butter, fluff, and sugar. Add the confectioners' sugar gradually, while beating. Add 1 teaspoon vanilla extract and mix so all ingredients are thoroughly combined. Transfer the filling to a pastry bag with a round tip. Pipe a dollop of filling on the flat side of half of the cooled cakes. Sandwich with remaining cookies.

CAKE

½ cup Dutch process cocoa powder

2½ cups quinoa flour mix (page 9)

1 teaspoon baking powder

1 teaspoon baking soda

½ teaspoon salt

1 stick unsalted butter, room temperature

1 cup sugar

1 large egg, room temperature

1 teaspoon vanilla extract

1 cup buttermilk (if you don't have buttermilk, you can make your own by mixing 1 cup of milk with 3½ teaspoons of lemon juice or white vinegar)

FILLING

½ cup (1 stick) unsalted butter

1 cup marshmallow fluff

1 cup confectioners' sugar

1 teaspoon vanilla extract

Pop Tarts

Makes about a dozen pop tarts.

Preheat oven to 350°F. Line a baking sheet with parchment paper.

In a large mixing bowl, whisk together the flour, xanthan gum, sugar, and salt. Add the melted butter, vanilla, and milk and mix. Use your hands to knead the dough until it hangs together and becomes smooth.

Line a flat work surface with parchment paper and dust with flour. Turn the dough onto the surface and place another piece of parchment paper over top. Roll out the dough to about ¼-inch thick. Peel away the top piece of parchment paper and slice dough into squares, hearts, or circles. Gather scraps into a ball, roll out again, and repeat until dough is all used up.

Spoon a little jam into the center of the pastry. Place another pastry cut-out on top. Use the back of a fork to seal the edges. Transfer to the lined baking sheet and bake for 8 to 10 minutes, or until the edges begin to turn golden. Transfer to wire rack to cool.

If you like your pop tarts sweeter, mix up some confectioners' sugar with a bit of milk or water and drizzle the glaze over the cooled pop tarts.

PASTRY

1½ cups quinoa flour mix (page 9)

½ teaspoon xanthan gum

¼ cup sugar

¼ teaspoon salt

4 tablespoons butter, melted

1 teaspoon vanilla extract

3 tablespoons milk

FILLING

6 tablespoons jam

Empanaditas

Makes about 10.

In a medium mixing bowl, beat together the butter and cream cheese. Gradually add the flour and cornmeal, beating at low speed, until all the flour is incorporated. Gather the dough into two balls, wrap each in plastic wrap, and refrigerate for at least 2 hours.

Heat oven to 375°F and grease a baking sheet. Place a large sheet of waxed paper on a flat work surface, place one ball of dough in the center, and lay a second sheet of waxed paper over the top. Roll out the dough to about ⅛-inch thick.

Cut dough into 3 x 3-inch squares. Spread a little dulce de leche on half the squares and place a few thin slices of banana on top. Cover with another pastry square and use a fork to seal the edges. Sprinkle with cinnamon sugar.

Bake for 12 to 15 minutes or until golden.

1 cup unsalted butter, softened
1 (8-ounce) package cream cheese, softened
1½ cups quinoa flour mix (page 9)
½ cup cornmeal
1 cup dulce de leche
2 medium bananas
Cinnamon sugar for sprinkling

Dulce de leche is a South American treat that is essentially caramelized milk. You can find it in specialty stores or online.

Summery Strawberry Crisp

Makes 8 to 10 servings.

Preheat oven to 350°F. Divide strawberries between 8 to 10 ramekins or place in a pie plate. To make the topping, combine oats, cooked quinoa, sugar, and butter and mix. Sprinkle evenly over strawberries. Bake for 20 to 30 minutes, or until tops are golden and berries are bubbly.

To make the whipped cream, beat all ingredients together until light and fluffy. Serve a dollop on each serving of crisp.

STRAWBERRY CRISP

¾ cup gluten-free oats

¾ cup cooked quinoa

½ cup sliced almonds

¾ cup brown sugar or
   coconut sugar

1 stick (½ cup) butter, softened

1 pound strawberries (fresh or
   frozen), hulls removed and sliced

WHIPPED CREAM

1 pint heavy whipping cream

1 teaspoon vanilla extract

1 teaspoon honey

Rhubarb Crumble

Makes 8 to 10 servings.

Preheat oven to 350°F.

In a saucepan, heat rhubarb and granulated sugar and simmer for about 10 minutes, or until the rhubarb starts to become soft. Remove from heat. Transfer to a pie plate.

To make the topping, combine oats, cooked quinoa, brown sugar, and butter and mix. Spread over cooked rhubarb. Bake for 20 to 30 minutes, or until top is golden.

3 cups chopped rhubarb

1 cup granulated sugar

¾ cup gluten-free oats

¾ cup cooked quinoa

¾ cup brown sugar or
    coconut sugar

1 stick (½ cup) butter, softened

For a variation, add some hulled and sliced strawberries or peach slices to the rhubarb after it has cooked!

142

Pies, Tarts, Crisps, and Crumbles

Blueberry Crumble

Makes 8 to 10 servings.

Preheat oven to 350°F.

Place blueberries in a 9-inch pie plate.

To make the topping, combine oats, cooked quinoa, almonds, sugar, and butter and mix. Spread over blueberries. Bake for 20 to 30 minutes, or until top is golden.

3 cups fresh or thawed blueberries
¾ cup gluten-free oats
¾ cup cooked quinoa
½ cup sliced almonds
¾ cup brown sugar or
    coconut sugar
1 stick (½ cup) butter, softened

Apple Pear Quinoa Crumble

Makes 8 servings.

Preheat oven to 400°F. Grease 8 six- to eight-ounce ramekins.

In a small bowl combine quinoa flour, quinoa, nuts, sugar, and cinnamon. Using a pastry cutter or the back of a fork mix in butter until coarse crumbs are formed.

In a large bowl combine pears and apples. Toss with sugar and flour. Add lemon juice and apple juice and stir until well combined. Place apple mixture in ramekins and top with streusel. Bake for 40 minutes.

½ cup toasted quinoa flour

½ cup cooked quinoa

¼ cup chopped walnuts
    or sliced almonds

¼ cup coconut palm sugar
    or brown sugar

¼ teaspoon ground cinnamon

3 tablespoons Earth Balance or
    butter, softened

3 medium apples, peeled
    and chopped

3 medium pears, peeled
    and chopped

2 tablespoons coconut palm sugar

1 tablespoon toasted quinoa flour

2 tablespoons lemon juice

¼ cup apple cider or apple juice

This recipe comes from *The Gluten-Free Quintessential Quinoa Cookbook* by Wendy Polisi.

Puddings and Other Sweet Treats

Lemon Coconut Pudding with Mangos

Makes 2 servings.

In a small saucepan, combine the quinoa and coconut milk and bring to a boil. Reduce to a simmer, cover, and stir occasionally for about half an hour. Remove from heat and add lemon juice and maple syrup. Allow to cool and then transfer to refrigerator to chill.

Layer pudding and mango chunks in a bowl or glass and sprinkle slivered almonds on top, if desired.

¾ cup uncooked quinoa

1 (14-ounce) can coconut milk

2 tablespoons lemon juice

2 tablespoons pure maple syrup

½ cup fresh or thawed mango chunks

Slivered almonds (optional)

I used tri-colored quinoa in the pudding shown here, but any color will do!

Cinnamon-Vanilla Pudding

Makes 4 servings.

In a small saucepan, combine the quinoa
and milk and bring to a boil. Reduce to
a simmer, cover, and stir occasionally
for about half an hour. Add maple syrup,
vanilla, and cinnamon, and stir. Serve warm
or chilled.

1 cup uncooked quinoa

3 cups milk

3 tablespoons pure maple syrup

1 teaspoon vanilla extract

1 teaspoon cinnamon

Chocolate Quinoa Porridge

Makes 12 servings.

Bring quinoa flakes or quinoa, cocoa powder, and water or milk to a simmer in a medium saucepan. Reduce heat and simmer for about 7 minutes, or until most of the liquid has absorbed. Stir occasionally to prevent sticking.

Add vanilla, dried cherries, sunflower seeds, and maple syrup and stir until heated through. Transfer to a serving bowl and garnish with cocoa nibs and strawberries.

$\frac{1}{3}$ cup quinoa flakes or cooked quinoa

$\frac{1}{2}$ tablespoon cocoa powder or cacao powder

$\frac{3}{4}$ cup water or milk of choice

1 teaspoon vanilla extract

1 tablespoon dried cherries

1 tablespoon sunflower seeds

1 tablespoon maple syrup

$\frac{1}{2}$ tablespoon cocoa nibs or chocolate chips

$\frac{1}{2}$ cup sliced strawberries

This recipe comes from *The Gluten-Free Quintessential Quinoa Cookbook* by Wendy Polisi.

Grilled Peaches with Maple Cinnamon Yogurt

Make 4 servings.

Heat greased grill to medium-high.

Mix together the yogurt, 1 tablespoon of the maple syrup, and the cinnamon. Set aside.

Wash the peaches, slice them in half, and remove the pits. Brush the cut sides with the remaining maple syrup. Grill cut-side down 6–8 minutes or until softened. Top with a dollop of the yogurt, sprinkle with the Quinoa Cashew Crunch 'n' Munch, and serve immediately.

4 peaches

3 tablespoons maple syrup, divided

½ cup Greek-style yogurt

¼ teaspoon ground cinnamon

¼ Quinoa Cashew Crunch 'n' Munch (page 157)

Berries & Quinoa with Vanilla Bean Syrup

Makes 6 servings.

Using a sharp paring knife, split the vanilla bean lengthwise. Scrape out seeds with the back of the knife, reserving the empty pod for a garnish if desired. Put the seeds in a small saucepan along with sugar and ¼ cup of water. Bring to simmer over medium heat, stirring until sugar dissolves. Reduce heat to low and cook for 8 minutes. Strain through a fine strainer (the one you use to drain quinoa will work well). Let cool. Refrigerate until chilled.

Wash the berries and dry. If using strawberries, cut into quarters. Mix berries with quinoa and toss with just enough syrup to coat.

½ vanilla bean

¼ cup evaporated cane juice (or sugar of choice)

4 cups fresh berries

2 cups cooked quinoa

This recipe comes from *The Gluten-Free Quintessential Quinoa Cookbook* by Wendy Polisi.

Quinoa Cashew Crunch 'n' Munch

Makes 12 servings.

To pop the quinoa, place coconut oil in a popcorn popper and allow to get warm. Add quinoa and cook about 5 minutes, until quinoa is lightly brown. Alternatively, pop the quinoa in a covered saucepan, shaking to prevent burning.

In a large heavy saucepan, bring agave nectar, butter, almond butter, sugar, sea salt, and water to a boil, stirring often. Remove from heat and stir in popcorn, cashews, apples, and quinoa.

Arrange mixture on rimmed baking sheets lined with parchment paper. Allow to set for at least 20 minutes.

1 cup popped quinoa

1/3 cup agave nectar, coconut nectar, or maple syrup

2 tablespoons Earth Balance or butter

1/3 cup almond butter

1/2 cup coconut palm sugar

1 teaspoon sea salt

2 tablespoons water

10 cups popped popcorn

1 cup chopped cashews

1/2 cup chopped dried apples

This recipe comes from *The Gluten-Free Quintessential Quinoa Cookbook* by Wendy Polisi.

Quinoa Fruit Salad

Makes 2 servings.

In a small bowl, whisk together the lime juice and honey or maple syrup. Add the ground ginger and fresh mint and stir.

Combine all fruit in a medium bowl, add the cooked quinoa, and mix. Pour the lime juice mixture over top and stir to coat.

Juice from 1 lime

1 teaspoon honey or maple syrup

¼ teaspoon ground ginger

1 teaspoon chopped fresh mint leaves

1 cup cooked quinoa, cooled

¼ cup favorite fresh berries, rinsed

¼ cup mango pieces

¼ cup peach slices or other favorite fruit

Quinoa and Fruit Pudding

Makes 4 servings.

Rinse the quinoa and then place in a saucepan with the coconut milk and bring to a boil. Reduce to a simmer, cover, and stir occasionally for about half an hour.

Meanwhile, in a food processor, blend together the bananas, cherries, vanilla, and cinnamon. Add mixture to the cooked quinoa.

Stir in chopped apple and apricots and serve.

1 cup quinoa, raw

2 cups coconut milk

2 bananas

½ cup dried cherries

1 teaspoon vanilla

1 teaspoon cinnamon

½ cup chopped apple

½ cup chopped dried apricots

Peach Coconut Flan

Makes 6 servings.

Rinse the quinoa thoroughly. In a medium saucepan, combine quinoa and 1 cup of coconut milk. Simmer for about half an hour, stirring occasionally. Heat the oven to 350°F.

Use an immersion blender or food processor to puree the quinoa, gradually adding the additional ¾ cup of coconut milk.

In a separate bowl, beat together the eggs, maple syrup, and vanilla. Add to the quinoa puree.

In a small saucepan, make caramel sauce: combine sugar with 2 tablespoons water and stir over high heat until mixture becomes light brown. Divide hot caramel between 6 greased muffin cups.

Divide the quinoa mixture between 6 muffin cups (pouring over the caramel) and cover muffin tin with aluminum foil. To make a water bath, place the muffin tin in a deep pan filled with enough water to cover halfway up the muffin tin. Place in oven and bake for about 45 minutes, or until the custard is set.

Allow to cool several minutes and then turn muffin tin upside down over a baking sheet to remove the custards, using a knife or spatula as necessary to loosen the edges. Garnish with fresh peach slices.

½ cup quinoa, raw
1¾ cups coconut milk, divided
4 eggs
¼ cup maple syrup
2 teaspoons vanilla extract
1 cup sugar
2 peaches

Mini Chocolate Waffles with Marshmallow-Strawberry Dipping Sauce

Makes about 2 dozen.

Begin heating the waffle iron. In a large mixing bowl, whisk together the flour, cocoa powder, sugar, salt, and baking powder.

In a separate bowl, whisk together the milk, eggs, and butter. Pour the wet ingredients into the dry ingredients and stir to combine.

When the waffle iron is hot, grease or spray the irons and then ladle on the batter. You'll be making regular-sized waffles and then cutting them into smaller pieces when they're done. Cook 3 to 5 minutes, or until waffles are golden. Repeat until all batter is used.

While waffles are cooling, prepare the dipping sauce simply by mixing together the fluff and jam.

Use a small cookie cutter in desired shape to cut the waffles into small pieces. Circles or hearts work better than intricate shapes. Waffle scraps can be used instead of cookies in a trifle.

Scoop dipping sauce into a small bowl, place on a larger plate, and arrange the waffles on the plate around the bowl.

WAFFLES

2 cups quinoa flour mix (page 9)

2 tablespoons cocoa powder

½ cup sugar

½ teaspoon salt

3 teaspoons baking powder

1½ cups milk

2 eggs

4 tablespoons butter, melted

DIPPING SAUCE

½ cup marshmallow fluff

½ cup strawberry jam

Make-Ahead
Mixes

Gluten-Free Mexican Brownie Mix

Makes enough mix to fill one pint jar and to make one 8" x 8" pan of brownies.

Stir together all the ingredients and pour into a glass pint jar or a sealable bag.

Include these directions with the mix: Preheat oven to 350°F and grease an 8" x 8" pan. Combine all of the mix with ½ cup unsalted butter or coconut oil, softened; 2 large eggs; and 1 teaspoon vanilla. Pour batter into prepared pan and bake for about 25 minutes. Cool in the pan for several minutes before cutting.

½ cup quinoa flour mix (page 9)

½ cup unsweetened cocoa powder

¼ teaspoon baking powder

¼ teaspoon salt

¾ cup sugar

½ teaspoon cinnamon

½ teaspoon chili powder or cayenne pepper

To make a regular brownie mix (instead of Mexican brownies), just omit the cinnamon and chili powder or cayenne pepper. You can also add ½ cup of chocolate chips to the mix for extra chocolaty brownies (though you may need a slightly larger jar to package it in).

Gluten-Free Peanut Butter Cookie Mix

Makes mix for a dozen cookies.

Combine all ingredients and package in a glass jar or sealable bag.

Include these instructions with the mix: Preheat oven to 375°F. Combine the mix with ½ cup butter or coconut oil, 1 egg, 1 teaspoon vanilla, and ½ cup salted natural peanut butter. Roll dough into small balls and place 2" apart on a cookie sheet. Bake for about 8 minutes or until cookies hang together. Cool cookies on cookie sheet for a few minutes before transferring to a wire rack.

1½ cups quinoa flour mix (page 9)
½ teaspoon baking soda
½ cup brown sugar
¼ cup white sugar
½ cup chocolate chips

Gluten-Free Muffin Mix

Makes mix for 12 regular muffins or 6 large muffins.

Stir together all the ingredients and pour into a glass pint jar or a sealable bag.

Include these directions with the mix: Preheat oven to 400°F and grease a 12-cup muffin tin. Combine all of the mix with 4 tablespoons unsalted butter or coconut oil, melted; 2 large eggs; 1 cup milk; and 1 teaspoon vanilla. Mix just until combined. Pour batter into prepared pan and bake for about 20 minutes, or until a toothpick inserted into the center of a muffin comes out clean.

2 cups quinoa flour mix (page 9)

½ teaspoon xanthan gum

½ teaspoon salt

1 tablespoon baking powder

½ cup brown sugar

1 teaspoon cinnamon

½ teaspoon nutmeg

½ cup dried apples or berries (optional)

Conversion Charts

OVEN TEMPERATURES

Fahrenheit	Celcius	Gas Mark
225°	110°	$\frac{1}{4}$
250°	120°	$\frac{1}{2}$
275°	140°	1
300°	150°	2
325°	160°	3
350°	180°	4
375°	190°	5
400°	200°	6
425°	220°	7
450°	230°	8

METRIC AND IMPERIAL CONVERSIONS

(These conversions are rounded for convenience)

Ingredient	Cups/Tablespoons/Teaspoons	Ounces	Grams/Milliliters
Amaranth, uncooked	1 cup	6.8 ounces	190 grams
Butter	1 cup=16 tablespoons= 2 sticks	8 ounces	230 grams
Cream cheese	1 tablespoon	0.5 ounce	14.5 grams
Cornstarch	1 tablespoon	0.3 ounce	8 grams
Flour, all-purpose (gluten-free)	1 cup/1 tablespoon	4.5 ounces/0.3 ounce	125 grams/8 grams
Flour, buckwheat	1 cup	4.25 ounces	120 grams
Flour, sorghum	1 cup	4.25 ounces	120 grams
Fruit, dried	1 cup	4 ounces	120 grams
Fruits or veggies, chopped	1 cup	5 to 7 ounces	145 to 200 grams
Fruits or veggies, puréed	1 cup	8.5 ounces	245 grams
Honey or maple syrup	1 tablespoon	.75 ounce	20 grams
Liquids: cream, milk, water, or juice	1 cup	8 fluid ounces	240 milliliters
Oats	1 cup	5.5 ounces	150 grams
Quinoa, uncooked	1 cup	6 ounces	170 grams
Salt	1 teaspoon	0.2 ounce	6 grams
Spices: cinnamon, cloves, ginger, or nutmeg (ground)	1 teaspoon	0.2 ounce	5 milliliters
Sugar, brown, firmly packed	1 cup	7 ounces	200 grams
Sugar, white	1 cup/1 tablespoon	7 ounces/0.5 ounce	200 grams/12.5 grams
Vanilla extract	1 teaspoon	0.2 ounce	4 grams

Other Books by Abigail R. Gehring

The Healthy Gluten-Free Diet

The Magic of Mini Pies

Gluten-Free Miniature Desserts

The Complete Juicer

The Little Book of Country Baking

Classic Candy

The Good Living Guide to Country Skills

Back to Basics

Homesteading

Self-Sufficiency

The Homesteading Handbook

The Back to Basics Handbook

The Self-Sufficiency Handbook

The Country Living Handbook

The Illustrated Encyclopedia of Country Living

The Ultimate Guide to Old Fashioned Country Skills

Odd Jobs

Dangerous Jobs

The Simple Joys of Grandparenting

Index

Index

My Favorite Quinoa Recipes

My Favorite Quinoa Recipes

My Favorite Quinoa Recipes

ALSO AVAILABLE

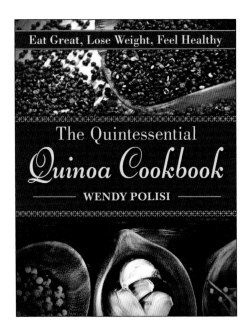

The Quintessential Quinoa Cookbook
Eat Great, Lose Weight, Feel Healthy

by Wendy Polisi

With over two-hundred pages of quinoa-inspired cuisine, *The Quintessential Quinoa Cookbook* is unlike any other quinoa cookbook. Inside you'll find Wendy's exclusive, handcrafted recipes, photographs of every recipe, nutritional information for every recipe, and alternative ingredients and preparation methods. Included are vegan, gluten-free, sugar-free, fast & easy, eating clean, kid-friendly, and even dessert quinoa recipes! Let's take a quick peek at the recipes included: Strawberry Spinach Quinoa Salad, Black Bean and Quinoa Tostadas, Quinoa Burgers, Almond Fudge Quinoa Brownies, Sun-Dried Tomato and Goat Cheese Pizza, and much more!

$17.95 Hardcover • ISBN 978-1-61608-535-3

ALSO AVAILABLE

Gluten-Free Miniature Desserts
Tartlets, Mini Pies, Cake Pops, and More

by Abigail R. Gehring

The only thing better than traditional dessert is an adorably small dessert you can pick up with your fingers and devour in a few sumptuous bites. Cake pops, mini pies, and tiny tarts are everyone's favorite new treats, and it's no wonder—they're cute, they're fun, and they're small enough that you can sample one of each at a party!

For the growing population with gluten allergies or sensitivity, dessert is tricky territory. Gehring, who has been gluten-free for three years, has experienced many of the pitfalls of gluten-free cooking and baking so you don't have to! Here are more than sixty recipes you'll have fun making and feel great eating:

- Banana Nutella Crepes
- Cherry Mascarpone Tartlets
- Chocolate Cheesecake Bonbons in Raspberry Sauce
- Chocolate Espresso Pots de Crème
- Coconut Key Lime Shooters
- Ginger Cream Tartlets
- Lemon Coconut Petit Fours
- Mini Chocolate Bundt Cakes with Sour Cream Glaze
- Pumpkin Whoopie Pies with Maple Cream Filling
- Raspberry Peach Cobbler

$14.95 Paperback • ISBN 978-1-62636-024-2

ALSO AVAILABLE

The Healthy Gluten-Free Diet
Nutritious and Delicious Recipes for a Gluten-Free Lifestyle

by Abigail R. Gehring

Fortunately for those with celiac disease or gluten-intolerance or sensitivity, gluten-free foods are becoming much more readily available at grocery stores and restaurants across the country. However, many prepackaged options are laden with sugar, unhealthy fats, and grains and starches that are devoid of nutritional value. They may be "safe" for those who can't eat gluten, but they're far from healthy. In *The Healthy Gluten-Free Diet*, Gehring provides nearly one hundred recipes that are safe for those on a gluten-free diet, healthy for anyone, and delicious for the whole family! Recipes include:

- Almond Flour Banana Bread
- Buckwheat Apple Pancakes
- Cheddar-Herb Drop Biscuits
- Cherry and Dark Chocolate Biscotti
- Grilled Pear Salad with Green Tea Dressing
- Moroccan Chickpea Slow Cooker Stew
- Oatmeal Peppermint Chip Cookies

- Polenta Feta Shrimp Bake
- Pumpkin Cornbread
- Quinoa Risotto with Shitake Mushrooms and Arugula
- Raspberry Peach Cobbler
- Sweet Potato Scones
- And many more!

Gehring loves experimenting with exciting grains and shares that thrill with her readers. Recipes utilize a variety of grains and flours including quinoa, millet, amaranth, teff, sorghum, brown rice, almond flour, coconut flour, and more. Learn the nutritional benefits of each and even discover how to grow, thresh, and grind your own grains!

$16.95 Hardcover • ISBN 978-1-62873-755-4